Demos is an independent think tank committed to radical thinking on the long-term problems facing the UK and other advanced industrial societies.

Demos
Panton House, 25 Haymarket, London SW1Y 4I
Tel: 0171 321 2200 Fax: 0171 321 2342
email: mail@demos.co.uk
www.demos.co.uk

The **ICA** is a public playground for exploring the shape of culture-to-come; for developing innovative art and new ideas; and for experimenting with the conditions under which young multicultural Britain encounters culture.

Institute of Contemporary Arts
The Mall, London SW1Y 5AH
Tel: 0171 930 0493 Fax: 0171 873 0051
email: info@ica.org.uk
www.ica.org.uk

The Smith Institute has been set up to look at issues flowing from the changing relationship between social values and economic imperatives, an area that was of particular interest to the late Rt Hon John Smith QC MP.

The Smith Institute
Victoria Station House, 191 Victoria Street, London SW1E 5NE
Tel: 0171 592 3629 Fax: 0171 828 9053
email: info@smith-institute.org.uk

The Independents
Britain's new cultural entrepreneurs

Charles Leadbeater and Kate Oakley

Demos   **Institute of Contemporary Arts**   **The Smith Institute**

First published in 1999 by
Demos
Panton House
25 Haymarket
London SW1Y 4EN
Telephone: 0171 321 2200
Facsimile: 0171 321 2342
email: mail@demos.co.uk

ISBN 1 898309 96 5
Printed in Great Britain by Redwood Books, Trowbridge
Design by Lindsay Nash

Contents

Acknowledgements

This research project is the result of a collaboration between Demos, the ICA and the Smith Institute.

The research was made possible by generous grants from the BBC; the Department of Trade and Industry; the Department for Culture, Media and Sport; the National Endowment of Science, Technology and the Arts; the Iron and Steel Trades Confederation; Sun Microsystems; Cap Gemini; and Sheffield Local Education Authority.

We are indebted to the wide range of people who agreed to be interviewed in the course of this research in Glasgow, Cardiff, Sheffield and Brighton. We interviewed people in local authorities, economic development agencies, large companies, universities and broadcasting as well as tens of cultural entrepreneurs running micro-businesses. We are grateful to them for the time they gave us.

We also benefited from talking to and reading the work of many people who have already written in this field, including Justin O'Connor at the Manchester Institute for Popular Culture, David Clarke of David Clarke Associates in Cardiff, Angela McRobbie and Scott Lash at Goldsmith's College, Phil Cooke at Cardiff University, Will Bell at the Arts Council of England and Kay Henning of Catalyst Media.

We would also like to thank Wilf Stevenson and Lizzie Mills at the Smith Institute and Philip Dodd at the ICA for their help in coordinating this project and the attendant seminars which, with the permission of Gordon Brown, the Chancellor of the Exchequer, were run in the summer of 1999 at Number 11 Downing Street.

Thanks also to Tom Bentley for helpful comments on earlier drafts of this report and Lindsay Nash who produced it.

1. The Independents

Aargh!

Deiniol Morris is very tired. In the last year he has had one week's holiday and he got that only thanks to an unforeseen delay in his latest project. Morris is an animator. He runs Aargh! Animation with Michael Mort, his business partner and fellow animator. Mort and Morris work from a unit on a nondescript industrial estate near Cardiff's docks. A handful of model-makers work in a darkened attic above the main workshop that houses the two studios where Morris and Mort make their films. Morris is typical of the new breed of young, independent, cultural entrepreneurs who are driving the growth of some of Britain's most dynamic industries: design, music, fashion, computer graphics and games, film and television. Morris' story exemplifies the opportunities and pressures as one of the new 'Independents'.

Morris left school at eighteen with an A-level in Art and then spent seven years playing in Welsh language rock bands. For much of this time he was on the dole. But rock music is a great training ground and through his bands Morris started working on graphics for pop videos. At the age of 24 he decided it was time to go to college. While studying for an arts foundation course in Bangor, Deiniol met some animators from Cardiff who recommended he should go to the Newport Film School, where he did a two-year Higher National Diploma in animation.

After leaving film school, Deiniol and a friend from one of his bands dreamt up the Gogs: the animated tale of a family of grunting cave dwellers who by chance discover fire. Through contacts in the rock business, Deiniol sold the Gogs idea to the commissioner for youth programmes at S4C, the Welsh language television channel. The first series of six five-minute films led to a second, which won critical acclaim as well as a contract to make an advertisement for Levi's. Deiniol and Michael were freelancers but became company directors when they created Aargh!. In 1998 they made a feature length animation with the BBC called Gogwana, as well as several other S4C animation projects.

By any standards, Deiniol Morris is a success. After a lacklustre time at school and a long spell of unemployment, he invested heavily in learning new skills, became self-employed and now runs his own business, which employs six staff full-time and as many as twenty freelancers when productions are in full-swing. The Gogs films have been sold to more than 60 countries and Aargh!'s work has won critical acclaim around the world. Morris is not rich but as an established animation director he earns more than many of his contemporaries. Yet life at Aargh! is anything but comfortable.

Like most of the new Independents, Deiniol and Michael are doing what they want to do but they are also caught in a bind. Aargh! is administered by a young production assistant who freely admits to being 'stressed-out'. The company's turnover is several hundred thousand pounds a year, but neither Deiniol nor Michael were trained in basic business skills, such as negotiating contracts, planning budgets or dealing with company finances. They acknowledge they need to hire a managing director, but finding the right person to work in such a tight knit and young company will not be easy. Even finding the time to address that issue is difficult. Aargh!'s income mainly comes from the fees it earns from making films; it does not earn much from royalties on its products. To keep Aargh! going Morris and Mort have to sustain this cash-flow, which means they are on a treadmill to deliver programmes to broadcasters. That leaves them little time to dream up the new ideas on which the company's future depends. Aargh!'s strengths and weaknesses are mirrored in thousands of young businesses created in the past decade by independents in the rapidly expanding cultural industries.

A growing share of the employment and output of some of the fastest growing sectors of the British economy is accounted for by this new breed of Independents. The government's Creative Industries Task Force estimated that the cultural industries generate revenues of £50 billion a year, employ 982,000 and generate value-added of about £25 billion

(4 per cent of gross domestic product) and had export earnings of £6.9 billion. These industries are growing at almost twice the rate of the economy as a whole, driven by powerful forces: cheaper and more powerful communications and computing, the spread of the Internet and growth in digital networks, which are opening up new distribution channels for small producers to serve global markets. As incomes and literacy levels rise around the world, so does the audience for English language services and content.

The Independents, like Morris and Mort, are a driving force of this growth. A large and growing share of employment in these industries is accounted for by the self-employed, freelancers and micro-businesses. These new Independents are often producers, designers, retailers and promoters all at the same time. They do not fit into neat categories. The Independents thrive on informal networks through which they organise work, often employing friends and former classmates. Although some are ambitious entrepreneurs, many want their businesses to stay small because they want to retain their independence and their focus on their creativity. Yet that does not mean they see themselves as artists who deserve public subsidy. They want to make their own way in the market. They have few tangible assets other than a couple of computers. They usually work from home or from nondescript and often run-down workshops. Their main assets are their creativity, skill, ingenuity and imagination. Across Britain there are thousands of young Independents working from bedrooms and garages, workshops and run-down offices, hoping that they will come up with the next Hotmail or Netscape, the next Lara Croft or Diddy Kong, the next Wallace and Gromit or *Notting Hill*.

Yet alongside the growth of this thriving ecology of small independents, two other trends are reshaping these cultural industries. One is the rapid pace of technological change, particularly digitalisation and the Internet, which is fundamentally altering how television, film software and entertainment will be distributed, stored and viewed. Another is the growing role of large companies, with global brands and reach, that increasingly dominate the distribution and publishing of commercial culture: Microsoft and Sony, Dreamworks and Disney, Time Warner and QVC. One of the aims of this report is to show how policy-makers can respond to give these young, often fragile companies a better chance of surviving amidst the swirl of these much larger forces. The capacity for the cultural industries, which are big exporters, to generate growth in jobs will in large part depend on whether this emerging base can be developed and strengthened to withstand the turbulence of the global markets upon which their output will increasingly depend.

One of the main findings of this research is that there is a large 'missing middle' in public policy at a national level and also, critically, at the regional and local level, where it most counts. Policy-makers know little about this new generation of entrepreneurs – how they work, where they come from, what makes them tick, their distinctive needs – nor how to interact with them. One of the chief aims of this report is to close that gap.

Based on dozens of interviews in Glasgow, Cardiff, Brighton and Sheffield, we have developed a profile of cultural entrepreneurs and the strengths and weaknesses of the businesses they create. We explore the milieu in which they thrive, which is often in cities and usually in networks that link them to larger organisations, such as broadcasters or commercial publishers and distributors. The report examines the different approaches of the four cities to the promotion of cultural entrepreneurs and draws conclusions about how national and local policy could be made more effective. First, however, we look at why this new generation of cultural entrepreneurs matter.

2. Why cultural entrepreneurs matter

It is all too easy to dismiss cultural entrepreneurs as marginal, fashion conscious and ephemeral: a distraction from the real business of manufacturing or financial services. The new Independents matter not just because they will be a source of jobs and growth in the future but also because they provide one model of how work and production is likely to change in the future in other sectors. Our research shows that cultural entrepreneurs matter for six main reasons, as set out below.

Jobs and growth

Cultural industries are increasingly important to the generation of new jobs and economic growth.[1] Even on modest assumptions of 4 to 5 per cent growth in these industries, twice the rate of the economy as a whole, they could employ 1.5 million and generate revenues of £80 billion, worth 6 per cent of gross domestic product, by the end the next decade. These estimates from the Creative Industries Task Force report are confirmed by our findings. The cultural industries employ between 2 and 8 per cent of the workforce in most British cities, rising to perhaps 10 per cent in London. To take Manchester as an example, a detailed analysis by the Manchester Institute of Popular Culture[2] found that 6 per cent of the Manchester workforce were employed in cultural industries, more than in construction and close to the scale of the long-established transport and communications sectors. The Independents account for perhaps two-thirds of the output of the faster growing sectors within the cultural economy.

Local economic growth

Cultural industries can create local sustainable jobs, which are less prey to the ups and downs of the global economy than, for example, jobs in branch offices and factories of large multinational companies.

Cultural industries are people intensive rather than capital intensive. They raise few of the environmental concerns that surround large industrial developments. Cultural entrepreneurs within a city or region tend to be densely interconnected. They trade with one another: pop bands need videos made, video makers need graphic designers. This high level of internal trade within the cultural industries means that an extra £100 of spending on the output of these industries will tend to generate more local jobs than an £100 spent on tradable commodities.

Cultural entrepreneurs, who often work within networks of collaborators within cities, are a good example of the economics of proximity. They thrive on easy access to local, tacit know-how – a style, a look, a sound – which is not accessible globally. Thus the cultural industries based on local know-how and skills show how cities can negotiate a new accommodation with the global market, in which cultural producers sell into much larger markets but rely upon a distinctive and defensible local base.

A new model of work

The Independents represent a vision of the future of work with new technology that is especially appealing to the young and could influence the development of other service industries in which self-employment and micro-businesses are growing.

In the 1980s it was commonplace to argue that new technology was creating a future in which capital would do without workers: workerless factories and paperless offices would usher in 'the end of work'. The Independents represent a quite different vision of the future of work: workers who want to do without capital.[3]

The Independents of the 1990s have emerged from a convergence of three forces:

Technology. This is the first generation that grew up with computers and that understands how to reap the benefits of modern computing power and communications. In earlier decades, increased computer power primarily benefited large organisations. The Independents feel enabled, not threatened, by new technology.

Values. The Independents were brought up by parents who were teenagers in the 1950s and 1960s, and they themselves became teenagers under Mrs Thatcher. They are anti-establishment, anti-traditionalist and in respects highly individualistic: they prize freedom, autonomy and choice. These values predispose them to pursue self-employment and entrepreneurship in a spirit of self-exploration and self-fulfilment.

Economics. The Independents came into the workforce in the late 1980s and 1990s as public subsidies to the arts were under pressure and many large commercial organisations were in the midst of downsizing. Careers in large organisations became more risky and uncertain: self-employment and entrepreneurship became a more realistic option.

These three factors – technology, values and economics – have converged to make self-employment and entrepreneurship a natural choice for young people in these industries. The risks that would have put off their parents do not daunt them. Their values encourage them towards entrepreneurship. The falling price of technology makes self-employment a real possibility. The crisis of employment in large organisations makes it a more attractive option.

Life as an Independent is not nirvana, nor even necessarily a recipe for making money. It can provide choice, autonomy and satisfaction but it also involves constant uncertainty, insecurity and change. Many young people find this trade-off of autonomy against insecurity more attractive than working for a large, impersonal organisation. The Independents have an approach to developing a career as a portfolio of projects, contacts and skills that may become increasingly important in other sectors of the economy.

A model of creative production

The Independents are developing a highly collaborative, creative and networked model of production, which shows how other industries could be organised in future. These businesses are built on the commercial application of creativity. That is why they may have much to teach companies in other industries, from retailing and consumer goods to software and biotechnology, in which competition is increasingly driven by innovation. The way cultural entrepreneurs organise their creativity carries lessons for other businesses. Independents have individualistic values but highly collaborative working practices. Their collaborative networks provide lessons for other sectors that are developing more networked forms of organisation, with more people working at home or as self-employed 'e-lancers'. The cultural industries are home to frequent job-hopping. Partnerships, bands and teams are formed and reformed. In the process ideas and skills get spread. The predominance of team-based project work means people have to learn how to trust one another very speedily. Other industries, in which large companies have predominated, may well have to come to learn these skills which seem intuitive to the Independents.

The future of cities

Cultural industries and entrepreneurs will play a critical role in reviving large cities that have suffered economic decline and dislocation over the past two decades. Culture is not just a source of jobs and income but also a sense of confidence and belonging. Cities that have invested successfully in cultural renewal do so to generate not just economic growth but also a renewed sense of civic pride and purpose.

Modern cities are nothing if they are not creative. They are centres for the largest and most diverse audiences for the consumption of culture and, as a result, cities are also home to the most productive clusters of cultural businesses. Cities attract newcomers and outsiders; they are places where people and ideas mix and mingle. They are places where knowledge and ideas are created, tested, shared, adapted and disseminated.[4] Policy towards the cultural industries is largely for and about cities. Cultural entrepreneurs will play two main roles in the regeneration of our larger cities.

Firstly, cultural entrepreneurs often take over offices, warehouses and factories left behind by the demise of older city-based industries. Employment in the cultural industries is primarily metropolitan: about 65 per cent of original production in cultural industries takes place in cities.[5] These industries thrive on a milieu that is itself creative and lively. Thus although the cultural industries do not, strictly speaking, include retailing, restaurants, hotels, bars and cafes, they can often create jobs in these sectors.

Secondly, cities that once based their identities around manufacture and trade are increasingly turning to sport and culture as a source of civic pride. Culture is increasingly central to how cities 'brand' themselves to attract students, inward investment and tourists. One of the most outstanding recent examples of this strategy is the transformation of Bilbao's international reputation with the building of Frank Gehry's Guggenheim Museum. Cultural entrepreneurship at the civic level will be critical to instil a renewed a sense of purpose, especially in cities that have been hollowed out by job losses and economic decline. To be effective, however, this demand-side approach to 'rebranding' a city with a new cultural image has to be matched by investment in indigenous production and business creation.

Social cohesion

Cultural entrepreneurs can play a critical role in promoting social cohesion and a sense of belonging. That is because art, culture and sport create meeting places for people in an increasingly diversified, fragmented and unequal society. Once these meeting places might have been provided by work, religion or trade unions.

Art and culture play a central role in some of the most impressive examples of social entrepreneurship, such as the Bromley-by-Bow project in the London's East End. Culture provided a central focus for the debate over Scottish identity in the run up to devolution, for example, through the opening of the National Museum of Scotland. Culture is often consumed publicly and jointly, it helps to provide a flow of shared experiences, language and images. For example, much modern pop music, and the fashion, language and style which goes with it, would be inconceivable without the influence of black music from which it sprang. Black people have probably had more influence on the dominant culture in Britain through pop music than any other channel.

Yet the growth of the cultural industries also poses some significant challenges in terms of social cohesion. Graduates make up a higher proportion of people in the youngest and fastest growing sectors than in other parts of the economy. Relatively few cultural entrepreneurs are from ethnic minority backgrounds. There is also a pronounced regional split in the distribution of jobs within these industries: London takes a far larger share of jobs in these industries than it does in other industries.

So although cultural consumption is critical to social cohesion, these cultural industries are less socially inclusive in terms of employment than other industries.

Conclusion: unrealised potential

The rise of the cultural entrepreneurs has exposed a serious shortfall in public policy. This is a classic example of how the speed of change in society – in technology, values, consumer habits and business organisation – frequently outpaces the capacity of public policy to learn, adapt and respond. Public policy is lagging behind for numerous reasons:

- Traditional arts and culture policy has focused on grant-giving to subsidised institutions for visual and performance arts. Traditional 'public' arts bodies know relatively little about commercial, cultural entrepreneurs, who are often suspicious of public subsidies. They want to prove themselves in the commercial market.
- Policy-making within local and national government is often split between 'culture' and 'economic development' departments that have different agendas.
- Policy-makers in economic development agencies – the Welsh Development Agency and the Scottish Development Agency, for example – are used to dealing with large inward investment projects that bring hundreds of jobs. They lack the knowledge, time and tools to help develop a cluster of hundreds of independent micro-businesses.
- Cultural entrepreneurs need to develop a mix of creative and business skills often at different stages of their careers. Education institutions are often too inflexible to deliver these skills as and when the entrepreneurs need them. The skills of cultural entrepreneurship, managing a rock band for example, can be learned but usually from experience and peers rather than in a classroom.
- Business advice and finance, for example through the Business Links scheme or via the banks, is tailored to the needs of mainstream businesses. Cultural entrepreneurs recognise they need busi-

ness advice but they want it from peers with whom they can identify rather than from 'men in suits' with little knowledge of these
new industries.

● Finance is often unavailable at the time and of the scale these entrepreneurs want. Often at the outset when they are developing their
ideas they need very small sums of money: a few thousand pounds
to buy some computers. That micro-credit is often hard to come by.
Later when they are hoping to develop their own products they
need a form of venture capital. Although venture capital has
become easier to access, many of these businesses find it hard to
raise.

This shortfall in the capacity of public policy is part of the 'missing
middle' – the institutions and policies that should stand between these
small businesses and the global companies they are often supplying.
Partly – but only partly – as a result of this shortfall, many cultural entrepreneurs run fragile, low-growth companies in industries that have low
barriers to entry and a high turnover of talent and ideas. Their businesses are often under-capitalised and lack the management skills and
bargaining power to deal with national and international publishers
and distributors. As a result many of these businesses do not realise their
full potential for growth.

3. Independent characters

Where did they come from?

The new cultural entrepreneurs have come in three waves. First, were independents in trades with a tradition of self-employment and small business, from architectural and design partnerships to rock bands. Second, were the generation of independent television producers created by the contracting out of television programme production in the 1980s, through Channel Four and the growing role of independent production within the BBC. Independent television companies have since branched out into film and radio, and also encouraged their own independent suppliers of graphics, music and set design. Broadcasters such as the BBC should play a critical role in developing and re-investing in this network. Third, a new generation of cultural entrepreneurs emerged in the 1990s, in multimedia, design, computer games, Internet services, fashion and music. These new entrepreneurs are less dependent than their 1980s counterparts on broadcasting. They are more international in outlook, more at home with digital technologies and happier to work across several media. They are often creators, producers, retailers, employers and public relations promoters all at the same time.

According to the government's Cultural Trends survey, about 34 per cent of people working in the cultural sector are self-employed, compared with an average of 15 per cent for the economy as a whole. Self-employment in the cultural sector rose by 81 per cent in the course of the 1980s, compared with 53 per cent in the economy as a whole.[6] Where people combine a job in the cultural sector with employment elsewhere, the rate of self-employment goes up to 65 per cent.[7] Temporary and seasonal employment is far more common in the cultural sector: 13 per cent of cultural sector employees are in tempo-rary jobs, twice the national average, rising to a fifth in film and televi-sion. That means close to 40 per cent of the workforce whose main job is in the cultural sector are in a form of self-employment and about 60 per cent of the workforce are either self-employed or work for a small busi-ness employing less than 25 people.

The workforce in these industries is disproportionately young: a third of people working in the cultural sector are aged between twenty and 34, compared with 26 per cent for the economy as a whole. The rate of self-employment is much higher in younger, newer sectors of the cultural industries and is lower in the subsidised and public cultural sectors, such as museums and galleries, which tend to have an older workforce. For example, about 30 per cent of the workforce in performing and visual arts, museums and libraries is over 50 years old, whereas a fifth of the workforce in the film industry is under 25. Employment in the cultural sector is split roughly equally between men (55 per cent) and women (45 per cent), although the proportion of women is higher in younger indus-tries. Ethnic minorities are under-represented in these industries.

The new independents are well educated. About 31 per cent were educated to degree level, and a further 12 per cent passed through other forms of higher education, a total of 43 per cent, compared with 22 per cent in the economy as a whole. Only 11 per cent of the workforce in these industries has qualifications equivalent to an 'O' level or less, a far lower proportion than for the economy as a whole. For younger people, higher education is increasingly the gateway to the newer more knowl-edge-intensive industries: 77 per cent of those between twenty and 34 in the cultural sector have a degree.

However higher education does not matter because degree courses provide people with formal training or skills in artistic production: only a tenth of people working in the cultural sector have formal creative arts qualifications. Higher education is important to the new Indepen-dents because a period at university allows them to experiment; univer-sity towns deliver large audiences for experimental, cheaply produced culture and cultural entrepreneurs often meet their future partners and collaborators at college. Universities are incubators for cultural entrepreneurs. Although these industries are still open to people with talent but no formal qualifications – the computer games industry is a prime example where young entrepreneurs have made it often because they decided not to go to university but to develop games instead – the scope for the talented non-graduate is dwindling. The expansion of higher education will play a vital role in opening up opportunities in these industries to all social groups.

Values and ambitions

'I decided early on that I did not want to work for anyone else and I have never had a job'
Stella Cardus, co founder Desktop Displays, Brighton

'Any business has to be well managed, including a creative one. If you cannot make the business stand up commercially you shouldn't be doing it.'
Janice Kirkpatrick, co-founder, Graven Images design studio, Glasgow

The new breed's most important characteristic is their sense of independence. Self-employment is rarely a stepping stone to employment in a larger organisation. Most people who are self-employed in the cultural sector want to stay that way. They do not want to work for large organisations: they recognise that employment has become more insecure and unstable; they do not want to be told what to do; they do not want to be part of a corporate culture or formal career structure; they prize their small scale as the basis for the intimate and creative character of their work. They opt for self-employment or micro-entrepreneurship because independence will give them a sense of authorship and ownership: it is the best way for them to develop their own work.

However, this antipathy to life in large organisations does not mean these independents want a life of leisure supported by public subsidy. On the contrary, they are often suspicious of public sector grants and subsidies, in part because these come with too many 'strings' attached. They want to prove themselves in the commercial market. They recognise that making it on their own, in the market, is perhaps a critical test of their ability, whether in pop, computer games, design or fashion. These independents are negotiating a space within the market economy where they can pursue their interests and develop their own products. Their acceptance of the market is pragmatic. They are not ideologically committed to it: they see it as the best way to pursue what they want to do.

Their attitude towards money is as ambivalent as their attitude to the market. In ways they are non-materialistic. They are prepared to earn relatively little – most people we interviewed were earning £10,000 to £20,000 a year – for long periods as the price of doing what they want to do. One example is Zap Productions, which started life by creating a famous Brighton nightclub and which now runs street-theatre productions. Zap has a turnover of £1 million a year. Its founder Dave Reeves pays himself £20,000 a year and his ten staff get about £12,000 a year. The Independents' offices are unfussy, functional and usually furnished from second hand furniture stores. But this does not mean that they are into 'art for art's sake'. They do not regard artistic poverty as a measure of creativity. Most say they would like to 'make it' and 'get rich'. They do not want to make their money by building organisational wealth in the form of a large company. Instead they want to 'have a hit' or 'be discovered'.

Very few of the entrepreneurs we interviewed had ever gone to the bank or outside investors to raise money. This is mainly because they assume outside finance would be too difficult to raise and too constraining on their freedom of action. Most are proud that they have funded their companies entirely from their own growth, although this can also heavily constrain their development.

'We've never been to a bank and never had an overdraft. We have funded our own expansion from our own income. If you run too fast and expand too quick you just see the good side of things, get over optimistic and don't see the crap coming towards you. We work hard and stay balanced.'
Peter Barker, Desktop Displays, Brighton

How they work

'The process inside our company is like sustained chaos. It's an intuitive process, which we can handle because we've been doing it for so long. But it's also vital to build relationships with customers so we really understand what they want and aspire to. It's not a soft culture: when

people come to work here we want them to challenge us and we want to challenge them. It's performance driven and we reward people with bonuses but its also cooperative and non-competitive.'
Janice Kirkpatrick, Graven Images

'Creative thought is at the heart of entrepreneurship.'
Dugald Cameron, Director, Glasgow School of Art

Cultural entrepreneurs opt for independence because it allows them to work in the way they want, which they would find hard to justify within a larger organisation. This mode of work is central to the way they generate and apply their creativity to commercial ends. The Independents are generally highly motivated and have a strong work ethic, although they do follow a traditional workday or week. They accept their work will be judged on performance, in competition with their peers. People are usually only as good as their last project. They work in a highly competitive environment, in which fashions and technologies can change very rapidly. Their approach to work is based on four ingredients.

- *They blur the demarcation line between consumption and production.* Creativity is only rarely a flash of brilliance that revolutionises an industry or a discipline. Creativity is more usually an incremental development that modifies and adapts what has gone before. That means a creative producer has to learn from a stream of complementary and competing products, which might provide ideas for their own work. Creativity in these industries is a constant process of borrowing and mixing. To be a creative producer it helps to be an avid consumer.
- *They blur the demarcation line between work and non-work.* As consumption and leisure are inputs into the creation of cultural products, the corollary is that periods not at work – leisure, relaxation, entertainment – can be as important as periods at work hunched over a computer terminal. Both contribute to delivering a creative product. Many of these independents say their best ideas come to them when they are not at work. Finding and justifying this 'downtime' is critical to any creative business. This carries lessons for

larger businesses that pride themselves on punishing work schedules for executives that leave little room for thinking and creating new ideas.

● *They combine individualistic values with collaborative working.* Cultural producers generally have a core discipline, for example, as a designer, director, camera operator or animator. These skills are their central contribution to the creative process. However they recognise their particular skill is next to useless unless it can be combined with the skills of others: producers, set designers, actors, musicians. Although there are plenty of prima donnas, these Independents accept collaborative team-working as the norm. They expect to work in teams; they collaborate to compete.

● *They are members of a wider creative community.* Creative communities can provide ideas, contacts, complementary skills, venues and access to the market. They induce a process of intense rivalry and competition as well as promoting cooperation and collaboration. These creative communities are invariably formed within cities, often around hubs: universities, arts centres, managed workspaces or broadcasters.

The independent business

'Graven Images is not going to get bigger. It is difficult to manage a big business well and remain creative. We want to concentrate on quality and apply our creativity in new settings. Business skills can be learned. What really matters is having creative skills and enjoying what you are doing. That is the important thing.'
Janice Kirkpatrick, co-founder Graven Images design studio, Glasgow

'Our aim remains to concentrate on doing really great work rather than growing the company just for the sake of making money.'
Alex Morrison, managing director, Cognitive Applications

'Britain is a nation of shopkeepers and that applies to these new industries as much as it does to older ones.'
Tim Carrigan, NoHo Digital

Cultural entrepreneurs believe in 'small is beautiful'. They generally run small, under-capitalised and quite fragile companies. They operate in fashion driven markets that are open to new entrants and in which new technologies are driving down the costs of production but also the prices that independents can charge for their services. They often lack and do not know how to acquire the business skills and support they need to grow a company.

There is nothing soft about life in these industries. These sectors are often chronically unstable and unpredictable. Given these pitfalls it is quite rational for Independents to want to stay small, not just for creative reasons but to avoid over-committing themselves. Given the diversity of cultural businesses it is impossible to describe a typical lifecycle that all such businesses pass through. The career of many cultural entrepreneurs is punctuated by success and failure, with periods of business expansions sometimes followed by a return to self-employment.

Many Internet-based companies, for example, believe they have a shelf life of perhaps only three years before having to completely change their business model and service. A leading Internet entrepreneur, Steve Bowbrick of Funmail, is a good example of the ups and downs an entrepreneur goes through in the new media industries. In the early 1990s Bowbrick created WebMedia, a successful website design company. But three subsequent ventures to create Internet information services failed and WebMedia folded, taking a substantial amount of venture capital with it. Bowbrick spent a year developing three ideas for Internet-based marketing products, none of which was successful, before hitting on the idea of Funmail, a new email product that proved hugely popular after its launch in the summer of 1999.

However, in general these entrepreneurs and the businesses they create seem to face three critical choices at critical junctures of their development.

Gestation

Independents often spend a lot of time (perhaps several years) early in their careers sorting out what they want to do, what their distinctive skill is and how they might make money from it. This period of exploration can be chaotic and unfocused but it is vital because often it is only the sense of vocation formed at this early stage that carries them through the uncertainties they will face later on. In this period cultural entrepreneurs often do not need business skills or large investments. They need quite small sums to keep going. At this stage they need access to micro-credit. At the moment the only institution providing such credit on a large scale is the Prince's Business Youth Trust, although the National Endowment for Science, Technology and the Arts has also entered the field.

Growth
Once a cultural entrepreneur has sorted out their marketable skill they have a chance to grow, usually by selling services and one-off projects. In this phase people can move from freelancing to setting up as sole traders and then create a micro-business.

Growth of these service-based businesses, in which people have to constantly find new customers, is difficult to sustain. It requires a considerable investment of time and management expertise to manage cash-flow. That means cultural entrepreneurs – now perhaps several years out of higher education – need to acquire basic business skills. They need to start formulating business plans and budgets. Businesses based on service provision often go through periods of feast, when they have a lot of work, followed by a famine: they have been so busy delivering their current projects they cannot find the time to sell new ones. In television this is becoming more difficult as budgets per hour of programming have generally been cut with the advent of digital technology, which should make production cheaper. Getting beyond this feast and famine cycle requires more sophisticated management to smooth the peaks and troughs of cash-flow. In this phase cultural entrepreneurs either have to acquire more basic business skills themselves or to recruit people with those skills. The entrepreneurs we interviewed often found it hard to do either.

'We used to concentrate on making all the films and documentaries ourselves. But then we realised we could be creative with the company rather than with the product. Rather than pursue an ambition to be a big director I decided to focus on building the company. We want to be able to develop our own content and own the rights. We want to go from

How to make it as an Independent

1. Be prepared to have several goes. You're unlikely to make it first time around. Learn from failure, don't wallow in it.

2. Timing is critical. Technology is moving so fast it's easy to be either too early or too late.

3. Don't have a plan: it will come unstuck because it's too inflexible.

4. Have an intuition and a feel for where the market is headed which can adapt and change with the consumers.

5. Be brave enough to be distinctive. If you are doing what everyone else is doing you're in the wrong business.

6. Be passionate: if you don't believe in what you are doing no one else will. At the outset only passion will persuade people to back you.

7. Keep your business lean. Buy top of the range computers but put them on second hand desks. Necessity is the mother of invention, not luxury.

8. Make work fun. If it stops being fun people will not be creative.

9. Give your employees a stake in the business: you may not be able to pay them much to start with so give them shares.

10. Pick partners who are as committed as you. To start with a business will only be sustained by a band of believers.

11. Be ready to split with your partners – often your best friends – when the business faces a crisis or a turning point. Don't be sentimental.

12. Create products that can become ubiquitous quickly, for example by being given away in a global market, thereby attracting huge stock market valuations.

13. Don't aim to become the next Bill Gates, aim to get bought out by him.

14. Take a holiday in Silicon Valley. You will be convinced anyone is capable of anything.

supplying a service to owning a product. But that is more complex, risky and time consuming.'
Hamish Barbour, co founder Ideal World, television and film production company, Glasgow

Own product development

The other option is to shift from providing a service to providing a product – films, music, designs, gadgets, computer games – from which a company can earn royalties. This process of investment in product development can be very risky without the backing of a major customer, and it can quickly consume a small company's resources.

The problems inherent in managing growth in a cultural business mean that most stay very small, rather than taking the risk and strain. Possibly 80 per cent of the Independents we interviewed were either self-employed or running a micro-business of no more than five people, with no ambitions for growth. A further 10 to 15 per cent were in the second phase: they were running a growing, service-based business. Only 5 to 10 per cent were in a position to contemplate going beyond that into own-product development and only a minority of these are likely to make it. The companies that can make it through these stages of development seem to be distinguished by these characteristics. They have:

- enough money to finance product development
- enough commercial discipline to make sure this investment is not wasted
- positions in potentially lucrative, international markets rather than small, national or niche markets
- unshakeable self-belief in their distinctive talent
- and last, but not least, luck.

This preponderance of self-employment, sole traders and micro-businesses in the cultural industries has important implications for policy-making. Government sponsored business support programmes and arts funding is tailored toward fewer larger organisations. Developing an ecology of hundreds of micro-businesses requires a set of policy tools that most economic development agencies lack. The danger is that we are creating industries dominated by 'digital craft producers', which in turn will be dominated by larger international groups that will control distribution and publishing of their products. These sectors will continue to generate jobs primarily by spawning more small businesses, but they also need to create larger, stronger, faster growth businesses that can operate in international markets. And we need to create stronger institutions and intermediaries that can support independent producers and stand between them and the global markets in which they compete.

4. Innovative cities

The lonely, existential genius does not exist in modern creative industries. It is virtually impossible for cultural entrepreneurs to work in isolation. Their skills and talents usually emerge from a creative community and they are sustained by a shared milieu. That is why cultural entrepreneurs congregate in cities: they provide the most creative milieu in which they can work. The ingredients of a creative milieu are difficult to define. People describe the atmosphere of a creative city in elusive but evocative terms.

The centre of Glasgow, for example, has a palpable buzz. At night its restaurants, bars, cafes and clubs are busy. By day it has galleries and designer shops. The city's striking Victorian buildings provide not just homes to designers and artists, they lend the place a kind of swagger, ambition and style. There is a seductive sense that something creative is afoot in downtown Glasgow: yet it is difficult to pin down where this 'buzz' comes from and what it amounts to. Critics argue it is an empty shell, a thin outer coating of over-hyped glitz that distracts attention from the unemployment and industrial decline that still dominate the city. A genuinely creative milieu is more than a collection of workshops, restaurants and bars, which are just the most superficial manifestations of a creative environment. An innovative milieu is a shared space and tradition in which people can learn, compare, compete and collaborate and through which ideas can be proposed, developed, disseminated and rejected. Watt's steam engine emerged from just such an innovative milieu in Glasgow in the last century, as did cotton spinning in Lancashire, Henry Ford's approach to mass manufacturing of cars in Detroit and the film industry in Los Angeles.

A genuinely creative milieu is more than just a lifestyle. It has to be judged by the quality and impact of its output as well. Cultural entrepreneurs have to be part of an innovative milieu to feed the creativity of their companies. To promote more successful cultural entrepreneurs we have to promote a creative environment within our cities. This environment will be critical to whether cities can sustain local jobs based on distinctive local know-how and skills.

Why an innovative milieu matters

Access to an innovative milieu is critical to cultural entrepreneurs for several reasons:

- producers need to publish and share their ideas through galleries, venues, exhibitions
- they need to share information about customers and to collaborate to exploit new opportunities
- a milieu creates a network of people with the complementary skills and assets needed to complete a project, for example, gathering a freelance crew to make an animated film
- networks are a way to embed in people the distinctive, shared tacit knowledge that makes up a distinctive style, sound or look for which a city can become known: the Mersey sound, Madchester, Britart in Hoxton
- independent producers need access to a supply of resources and skills in the form of public institutions, universities and colleges
- they also need agents, brokers or promoters who will give them access to the market beyond their locality: a dynamic milieu cannot be closed or inward looking.

A creative milieu is like a public good. No single cultural entrepreneur or institution can hope to create, manage or control it. Instead, these environments develop through complementary investments and commitments from multiple sources, which have spill-over benefits for all concerned. An innovative milieu is like a shared habitat or ecology.

Our research in Glasgow, Cardiff, Sheffield and Brighton, as well as research on cities such as Manchester and Barcelona, highlights several steps cities can take to promote cultural industries. Detailed case studies of these cities are set out in the appendix. Each has adopted quite distinctive approaches, developing distinctive strengths. In Sheffield, for example, the focus has been on using public investment to promote job creation in the Cultural Industries Quarter. In Glasgow, the local authority has played a leading role in using culture to reinvent the city's reputation, for example through, the European City of Culture Year in 1990 and the 1999 Year of Design and Architecture. This strategy has come in for a lot of criticism but has also encouraged a decade-long process of learning and adaptation that has strengthened the city's capacity to engage in these industries. Cardiff, by contrast, is a much smaller city than Glasgow but a capital nonetheless. Its municipal leaders have given far less weight to culture and its cultural institutions are far less engaged with the economy than in Glasgow. However, the strength of the media sector in Cardiff, in which the BBC and public funding plays a critical role, is an interesting model of how a cultural industry cluster can develop. Finally, Brighton has exploited its proximity to London to market itself as a lifestyle economy, attracting a community of small-scale producers, many of them working in visual arts and new media. This creative community, although mainly made up of fragile Independents, shows signs of developing a self-sustaining momentum.

The main message from these four cities is that cities are nothing if they are not creative. In the nineteenth century it was commonplace for cities to be seen as either industrial and commercial or artistic and political. In the coming century those distinctions will dissolve: cities will have to be commercial by being creative. Cities are spawning grounds for new ideas. Cities that once based their wealth and identity on trade, manufacturing or even basic service industries are having to reinvent themselves. That search for a renewed sense of purpose has led many cities to promote their culture to attract both consumers and producers. This effort to develop creative cities raises some critical questions.

- What are the components – public and private, formal and informal – of a 'creative city'?
- What role can public policy play in promoting a thriving cultural industries sector?

- Can cities really compete in the cultural economy from a provincial base?
- Can the cultural industries, which are often seen as fashionable if not élitist, play a role in combating poverty and social exclusion, or are they simply a diversion from the deep-seated social problems which beset many large cities?

Our research in Glasgow, Cardiff, Brighton and Sheffield suggests the following lessons for cities seeking to promote their creativity.

Places. Cultural entrepreneurs need flexible cheap places where they can work: workshops and offices in old warehouses, office blocks, converted schools, banks and chapels. Cheap space is a vital ingredient: that is why young cultural entrepreneurs will often work in run-down areas where more traditional businesses fear to tread. Independent producers also need places where they can display their work – venues and galleries – as well as places where they can meet and socialise, in bars, pubs and clubs. Providers of managed workspaces, such as Citibase, are moving into this area, but there are also excellent examples – the Chapter Arts Centre in Cardiff is one – of how managed workspaces designed to develop and spin-off businesses can be publicly supported.

Deregulation. Providing a set of spaces is just the starting point: what matters is what people do in these shared spaces. While local authorities can help to provide workplaces, the creative atmosphere of downtown city areas emerges from deregulation and experimentation. The fashionable art scene in London's East End neighbourhood of Hoxton has had very little to do with public policy. The most important ingredient was the availability of large, cheap warehouse space, combined with a string of cheap bars and restaurants. Deregulation to create an open, lively, diverse atmosphere is as important as public investment in managed workspace.

Density. An innovative milieu requires a high density of communication and interaction to allow people to rapidly share, copy, learn and modify ideas. Aspects of this can be mimicked by electronic networks which are being used, for example, to link together artists and designers in the

Highland and Islands of Scotland. However, this is one reason why cultural entrepreneurs will tend to congregate in cities and towns, and prefer mixed-use neighbourhoods in which they can work, socialise and live. Canton in Cardiff is an example of just such a neighbourhood as is the Merchant City within Glasgow. This social interaction is helped of course by prosaic things like good public transport links and crime prevention programmes. One of the biggest problems cited by musicians and clubs in Manchester, for example, is the influence of organised crime.

History matters. It is impossible to develop a cultural base from scratch. Not only does a city need strong cultural and educational institutions, it also needs to draw upon a cultural tradition for its output to be distinctive. An innovative milieu is not a lifestyle and it must be more enduring than a series of high-profile cultural events designed to lure visitors to a city's galleries and museums. Cultural producers thrive within, and often in opposition to, a cultural tradition that gives them access to skills and know-how as well as a sense of identity and purpose.

A creative milieu transmits distinctive skills and tacit knowledge that are difficult for outsiders to imitate. The distinctive knowledge-base has to be fed by local traditions of learning and skill, for example the traditions of architecture, fine arts and engineering of Glasgow. Liverpool, Manchester and South Wales, all have distinctive informal 'schools' that have promoted innovation in pop music. In Cardiff cultural production is inextricably connected to the debate over how the region should respond to decline in its coal, steel and manufacturing industries, as well as the contested role of the Welsh language. An area's creativity often emerges from a sense of contest over its identity and what it stands for. Creative places are rarely settled and cosy; they are usually in the midst of battles between 'old' and 'new' sources of wealth, income and identity.

Consumption and production are best developed in tandem. A purely 'production led' strategy will not engage the public, attract tourism or create the 'buzz' that has helped, for example, to give the centre of Glasgow a sense of renewed life. This is one shortcoming of Sheffield's investment in cultural production rather than consumption. However, a purely consumption-based strategy – which relies on events or the opening of new venues and attractions – will make only a limited contribution to developing the capacity of firms in the local economy to innovate and add value.

A thriving 'scene' is not necessarily a thriving industry. Cultural producers, whether musicians, artists or designers, generally emerge from a vibrant, competitive local scene, which helps to sustain them. Yet the presence of a thriving scene does not mean a city will prosper from its local talent unless it also has a business infrastructure of publishers, managers and distributors. An innovative milieu has to be creative but also commercial. The strongest creative clusters combine production with distribution, publishing, marketing and finance. For example, Los Angeles dominates the film business because that is where most of the money and most of the talent congregates. An innovative milieu cannot be based on a narrow, thin local market. In most UK cities, no matter how creative, this commercial ingredient is missing or rather access to it lies with large international distributors and publishers based in London. Just because an area has a thriving local *scene* does not mean it has a thriving local *industry*. South Wales, for example, has a thriving pop music scene, with lots of talented bands and venues inspired by the success of the Manic Street Preachers, Stereophonics and Catatonia. However the region does not have a pop music industry to speak of: employment in publishing, management, distribution and marketing are all concentrated in London. Cultural industry strategies usually focus on developing a local production base. In future they will have to pay more attention to how regional cities can retain more of the economic benefits from the downstream, commercial activities that their talent base generates.

A good example of how this can be done is the role that Chris Grace at S4C, the Welsh language broadcasting company, has played in developing the animation cluster in Cardiff by helping to take its products to international markets. Grace is an exemplary intermediary and entrepreneur who has exploited a niche for animation of world classics, such as the Oscar nominated Canterbury Tales.

New ideas and people. A creative milieu needs to be fed by a stream of new ideas and talents. That is another reason these innovative environments develop in cities that attract young people, immigrants and outsiders. A large city embraces a far greater diversity of cultures and outlooks than a rural town, for example. Cities have to open up channels for new people to come and go. Closed cities are rarely highly creative. One such route to attract incoming talent is higher education.

Creative cities are education cities. Universities help provide a city with a stream of talent and ideas. In Glasgow, for example, the Glasgow School of Art and the Royal College of Drama and Music symbolise the city's artistic tradition and help attract creative young people to the city for their formal training. Universities also provide a large, ready audience for cheap, often experimental, music, art, video and design. Universities provide a channel through which young people can migrate to a city. The people they attract might stay in a city after their degree as part of the new independent sector. This is more important than providing formal training in cultural industries. Glasgow, for example, with a student population of close to 95,000, almost a sixth of its population, is thus far better placed to compete in these industries than Cardiff, which has a student population of just 17,000.

Creative cities need diverse sources of initiative. The most impressive cities are those in which different players have taken the lead at different times, with the baton passing from the council to the private sector, broadcasters and grassroots entrepreneurs. Reliance on a single actor or leader, whether public or private, will lead inevitably to unbalanced development. Investment in cultural industries is a cumulative process, which requires policy-makers to be flexible rather than stuck on a fixed plan.

The best example of this is the contrast between Sheffield and Glasgow. In Glasgow, for example, various players have taken the lead in the cultural sector's development. The city council was a vital player in initiatives such as the year-long European City of Culture in 1990 and the 1999 UK City of Architecture and Design, which have promoted Glasgow's image as a cultural centre. However the largest cultural festival in Glasgow, the West End Festival, which has filled the gap created by the demise of uneconomic, officially sponsored festivals, is run by an independent cultural entrepreneur, Michael Dale, who works from a theatre based in a converted church. The economic development of knowledge-based industries turns in part on the work of public bodies such as Scottish Enterprise and the Glasgow Development Authority. Meanwhile a new generation of Independents has emerged in Glasgow in the 1990s, led by companies such as Ideal World, in film and television; Graven Images, in design; Wigwam Digital, in multimedia; Red Lemon, in computer games; and Nairn's, in food and restaurants. This recent wave of cultural entrepreneurship builds on the solid foundations provided by institutions such as the Glasgow School of Art and the BBC's production base in the city. When these different players can be combined they have the chance to undertake quite ambitious developments that none could achieve on their own. The city council, for example, is keen to develop the Candelriggs area of the city as a music quarter. This will involve partnerships with property developers and the BBC as an anchor tenant, as well as the creation of recording studios, bars and venues that build upon the clutch of restaurants and design studios in the area.

In contrast, Sheffield's strategy has relied heavily on the local authority and one department within it. This risks distorting the development because many of the businesses are reliant on public subsidy and leaves the cultural initiative vulnerable to a change of political priorities.

Official 'cultural' institutions matter but what really counts is how they act. The presence of formal, public cultural institutions – museums, galleries, orchestras – can give a city a solid cultural base, but these institutions are often poorly connected to the entrepreneurial cultural economy. (This criticism has been made for example of the Welsh National Opera and the National Orchestra of Wales in Cardiff.) What matters is whether these institutions make the most of those connections. That often depends on a city having a sense of strategy articulated by its political leaders, as well as the leaders of these institutions engaging with the community.

Public policy leadership is critical but on its own not enough. Cities need to promote their cultural strengths to outsiders but also to their own people to encourage a shift in attitudes and outlook. Politicians play a critical role in this. But public policy, on its own, cannot create such a milieu. Public policy makers – local authorities, central government funding for the arts, economic development agencies, regeneration projects – can make at least five critical contributions through:

- branding and external promotion to lend a city a new reputation and change its sense of itself
- leading strategic investment in property development with other partners to redevelop run-down areas as centres for cultural production
- investing in cultural assets – museums, galleries, theatres, opera houses, events – that can help to win a city a reputation as a centre of culture
- licensing culture by allowing bars, cafés and clubs to develop
- providing an infrastructure – particularly of public transport and community safety – that allows people to move around a city easily at night.

Broadcasters are hubs of the cultural economy. A city's chances of sustaining a local base are helped enormously if it is home to a broadcaster. The BBC in particular will play a critical role as an intermediary in developing local cultural industries. Broadcasters such as the BBC remain important centres of production: they are significant cultural enterprises in their own right, directly supporting orchestras, drama, film and pop music. With a growing share of television production contracted out to independent producers, the broadcasters – the BBC, Channel 4 and the regional ITV companies – have become joint-investors in some of the most important aspects of the urban cultural economy.

A broadcaster can help to give the cultural industries within a city the ballast to resist the pull of London by:

- providing local producers with access to wider markets
- attracting, training and retaining people with skills
- providing content producers with the complementary marketing and financial skills they often lack
- helping to arrange co-finance for projects

- working with other institutions – universities, colleges and local councils – to build a brand reputation for a locality.

The future of large parts of the cultural industries will turn on how broadcasters and independent producers develop in partnership, to strengthen the local production base and a city's reputation for cultural innovation. All this will be in the midst of the changes sweeping the industry brought on by the advent of digital technology, which will change how programmes will be made, distributed and stored, and the character of their content.

Making the most of London. The most dynamic cities are not frightened of London's dominance but know how to make the most of having a global city at the heart of cultural commerce only a few hundred miles away. Most provincial British cities lack the scale and clout to compete with global centres of cultural production such as London, Los Angeles, New York and Paris. The first aim should be to stop cities losing their talent to London. The second is to strengthen the bargaining position of local producers in relation to international companies. That will require cities to form a more productive relationship with London as a global centre of cultural production.

Promoting indigenous role models. The final component is perhaps the most important: a city needs to develop an entrepreneurial culture, with indigenous role models of entrepreneurial success and risk taking. Glasgow and Manchester, for example, seem to have stronger risk taking cultures than Cardiff, a capital city with strong institutions of government, and Sheffield, with its traditions of trade unionism and Labour politics.

5. Promoting cultural enterprise

The cultural industries are fashionable sectors with low entry barriers that attract young entrepreneurs. In that sense these industries are thriving without any significantly new public policy interventions. The main aim of policy should be to create a conducive environment of education, business finance and open markets, which will give this sea of small producers a better chance of surviving and growing. One of the main aims of public policy should be to fill in the 'missing middle' between the small cultural entrepreneurs and the global companies that dominate the major markets and distribution channels for these products.

The gap between the pace of development in these new industries and the capacity of public policy to respond to these emerging trends means that the full potential of entrepreneurs in these new industries is probably not being exploited. This chapter sets out some practical steps public policy makers could take to achieve three policy goals:

- help more cultural entrepreneurs create viable businesses, promoting a more sustainable local ecology of micro-businesses
- encourage more cultural entrepreneurs to adopt more ambitious plans to grow their businesses
- extend opportunities for entrepreneurship so that they are open to talent and creativity from all sectors of society.

The achievement of these policy goals will involve changes in our approach to education, finance and business support, as well as involving broadcasters and local authorities. It will involve a multiplicity of sometimes small but reinforcing steps taken by these different players.

Education

Delivery of the core curriculum to improve standards of literacy and numeracy is vital. No one will be able to compete in the knowledge driven economy without being able to write, read and compute basic sums.

However, in parallel with the core curriculum we need to develop a creative curriculum that would be designed to encourage young people to learn flexibility, team work, problem solving, innovation and risk taking. This creative curriculum is not the same as teaching music, drama and art. It would focus instead on developing young people's capabilities to work flexibly, cope with change and act entrepreneurially. The National Foundation for the Teaching of Entrepreneurship in the US has developed some successful models in which young people learn skills through working in entrepreneurial teams to create mini-businesses. As one guide to what is happening elsewhere, the government labour force plan for Singapore to the year 2020 includes plans that 'teaching creativity' should take up one third of the curriculum.

Our research underlined how vital access to higher education is for future cultural entrepreneurs. Universities are incubators for cultural entrepreneurs. Expanding the reach of university education from the current 35 per cent of the eighteen year olds to more than 50 per cent will be vital to expand opportunity. This is more important than investing more in specialist institutions of artistic training.

Cultural entrepreneurs need to acquire business skills, but as and when and how they want to. Provision of training in these skills should be modular, flexible and demand led. Often cultural entrepreneurs do not realise they need these skills until long after they have left college and started a business. That is why these additional and top-up skills need to be delivered in a flexible way, using distance learning and often taught by peers.

This means that institutions of higher education have to become far more flexible and modular in the way they engage students in learning. One possibility would be for students to become members of a university or college, to which they could return for further education and training throughout their twenties, or indeed throughout their life. As Shona Reid, the incoming director of the Glasgow School of Art put it: 'Perhaps we need to think of educational institutions as being more like sets of relationships and flows of people, rather than as bricks and mortar and courses.'

The forms of collaboration and learning that exemplify the skills and qualities needed for success in the cultural and entrepreneurial economy often emerge at the edges of an institution's main business. This raises questions about how a college's or university's contribution and achievement are assessed. The research assessment exercises, teaching assessments and productivity measures are based on distant, national formulae. These measures miss the informal, fine grained and network-based forms of educational practice and innovation, which encourage spin-offs, cross-sectoral collaboration and risk taking.

The application and transfer of knowledge from one setting to another is often at the heart of entrepreneurship but it is too little encouraged or assessed within education. We also need better measurement of the contribution and interrelationship of education institutions and their surrounding economies. Too much effort is focused on understanding the financial flows up and down within the education sector. There is too little focus on the multiplier effects and return over time of a university acting as a hub for an area's industry.

A further goal, to be pursued through the ESRC and other funding councils, is to improve the quality of university research into the success and failure of different strategies in new media industries. Most business schools should follow the lead of the London Business School, which is developing a new media business programme.

Finance and business advice

Cultural entrepreneurs need different kinds of finance at different stages of their career.

At the earliest stages – prior to forming a fully-fledged business – cultural entrepreneurs often spend quite a long time developing a sense of their distinctive skill and product. During this phase they often need only very small amounts of money, measured in the low thousands of pounds – to buy a computer for example – to sustain them. There is a case for a new approach to public investment in cultural entrepreneurship. This would entail a shift in public arts funding away from grants to large institutions and towards smaller investments in cultural entrepreneurs, which would earn a rate of return, albeit not necessarily a commercial one. One possibility would be for the Arts Council and the National Endowment for Science, Technology and the Arts to underpin a revolving micro-credit fund for cultural entrepreneurs. This would have to be locally administered, by investors with local know-how, against quite hard edged criteria to minimise waste.

The other main need is for finance at latter stages of growth when established companies want to move into their own product development. This shift from financing a business from retained income to attracting outside investment is often risky for companies. There is little quantitative evidence on whether these young businesses in new fields face particular difficulties raising loans from banks in addition to those which other small businesses complain of. One possibility would be for the DTI and the Treasury to work in conjunction with the main British banks to examine best practice in lending to the cultural and new media businesses. A further possibility would be to redirect some public spending from inward investment projects towards building up cultural industries.

Cultural intermediaries and incubators

The supply of funding is only one problem. More important perhaps is the lack of appetite for it on the part of cultural entrepreneurs and a lack of understanding on the part of the financial community about the risks of cultural businesses. Intermediaries, such as Services to Software in Scotland, can play a critical role in helping to bridge the gap between these young entrepreneurs and potential financiers.

Finding ways to link these entrepreneurs to managers and advisers with more established business skills is also critical. This should be a role for the DTI's Business Link network but it is viewed by young entrepreneurs as too mainstream. The most effective approach might be for the government, through a challenge fund, to sponsor the creation of new cultural industries incubators or cultural intermediaries, like the Chapter Arts complex in Cardiff, which can help cultural businesses with workspace, business advice and access to finance. One aim would be for the government to sponsor, with local authorities, private investors and the arts councils, the creation of twenty cultural business incubators across Britain within the next three years.

Cultural intermediaries will be vital to fill in the 'missing middle' in the British cultural industries. Cultural intermediaries seek and promote new talent, circulate ideas and trends, put people in touch with one another, set up venues and provide access to commercial deals and a wider market. Cultural intermediaries are often former content producers who have moved on: rock singers turned managers, actors turned promoters, television programme makers turned commissioning editors. They oil the wheels of a city's cultural industries. In Silicon Valley, this role as the junction box of the region, where ideas and money meet, is played by venture capitalists. Cultural intermediaries are far less formal and far less powerful than venture capitalists, but like venture capitalists they are deal makers: in essence they take local talent to a wider commercial market. Thriving cultural sectors need not just creative producers but effective intermediaries as well. Promoting these intermediaries should become a goal of public policy.

In Cardiff, one of the best examples is the Chapter Arts Centre. Set up in 1971 in an old school by a group of artists, the centre soon attracted people from theatre, film, television and other arts. It provides 50 managed workspaces for about 150 people, as well as a café, bar, theatre and cinema. The key to Chapter's success is that it provides far more than simply workspaces. The centre's staff work with the artists and producers to help bid for funds, stage shows, find partners and develop business plans. To win a space in the oversubscribed building a project has to be both innovative and stand a chance of commercial self-sufficiency. Jannek Alexander, the centre's director, estimates there is a 10 per cent a year turnover of businesses. 'Five per cent leave because they fail and 5 per cent because they are successful enough to stand on their own.'

Nearby, Cultural Enterprise Services (CES), a consultancy run by former Chapter director David Clarke, helps cultural businesses draw up and implement their business plans. The network around Chapter now includes internationally successful animators, writers and film makers, all connected through the centre and CES, which facilitates joint working and networking. Since its inception several hundred cultural and media businesses have been spun out from Chapter to operate elsewhere in Cardiff. Chapter is an outstanding example of how a cultural business incubator should work. Although it is mainly funded by the Arts Council of Wales and European grants, Alexander explained its strength was its local knowledge: 'The big public agencies are too cumbersome and distant to engage in this kind of work effectively.'

In Glasgow, one of the most promising attempts to create a cultural intermediary is the Research Centre, set up by Channel Four. The centre, housed in Channel Four's Glasgow offices, is designed to help under-capitalised and under-resourced independent producers to develop business plans, manage their cash-flow and invest more in their own research and development. It provides a home for researchers from fledgling independents to work on programmes and aims to help television-based companies to extend their reach into multimedia. John McVay, who runs the centre explained: 'These young entrepreneurs are tough, resilient and hard working but few of them have the business skills they need. We want to work with young companies which Channel Four wants to give repeat commissions to which need to build up their business.' The centre, which serves independents in Wales and Northern Ireland as well as Scotland, may also directly invest in talented young producers with the aim of helping them to work in their home town rather than moving to London.

In Brighton, the Media Centre, a self-help initiative among local producers, is cited by many new media companies as a reason they will continue to work in the town. In Sheffield, the Workstation is a managed workspace, though says it works informally as an incubator. There are about 63 organisations in the Workstation, mostly small commercial companies. The majority of recent tenants are in new media and are often one or two person companies.

Broadcasters

It is difficult to overstate how critical broadcasters such as the BBC and Channel Four are to the future of the cultural industries in the UK. They are important centres of production, training and skills but they also help to create the national and international markets for independent producers. Their activities stretch from film and drama into education and on-line services. Critically, they are home to the marketing, branding and commercial skills that so many cultural entrepreneurs lack. As a result of public policy Britain has some media brands and organisations – the BBC is a leading example as is Channel Four in film – with recognition in the international marketplace. The broadcasters are at the heart of policy and strategy in these new cultural industries.

How the broadcasters develop their role will be critical to the growing band of independent producers that rely on them to some degree. More programmes are likely to be commissioned from independent producers. The BBC and Channel Four both have plans to increase the use of external suppliers, especially from the regions. The broadcasters have a vital role in helping to manage the development of the independent production base.

This is a complex task but three points stand out:

(i)   The relationship between the broadcasters and the independent producers needs to evolve, possibly quite radically. Two decades ago most television production was undertaken by broadcasters in integrated and hierarchical companies. Now there is more of an open market in which independent producers can pitch ideas to make programmes. This evolution from hierarchical organisation to a market-based model needs to go through a further stage of evolution in which the broadcasters build stronger relationship with their suppliers. This will mean moving from a primarily arm's length relationship to one that is based on partnership and joint investment. The broadcasters will have to see themselves as both consumers of the output of independent producers and investors in the independent production base. This close relationship will be essential for the broadcasters and producers to share information, know-how and risks, and to cope with the technological and other changes set to sweep the industry with the onset of digitalisation. Left to their own devices, not enough of the independent production companies (especially those outside London) have the capacity to innovate and adapt to radically new technologies. Broadcasters need to help build the capacity of the Independents on which they increasingly depend. That is why initiatives such as the Channel Four's Research Centre could provide a model for the future.

(ii) Broadcasters need to start reinvesting in the talent base that will provide the programme makers of the future. Many of the current generation of Independents were themselves trained while working for broadcasters in the 1980s. However, very few of the independent producers have enough spare capacity and resources to invest in training and developing new talent themselves. It is simply too costly and risky in businesses that work with short-term contracts and high staff turnover. As a result the broadcasters may have to start reinvesting directly, perhaps through scholarship programmes, in developing fledgling producers, especially in the regions.

(iii) The older generation of independent producers is predominantly television companies, many of them set up by former employees of large broadcasters. The younger generation of Independents is quite different. They will increasingly see themselves as entertainment software providers, who can provide content not just for television but also for computer games and multimedia applications. Again, the broadcasters will have a critical role to play in helping Independents to navigate their way through changes in technologies and markets.

It should become part of the licence obligation of publicly regulated broadcasters such as the BBC and Channel Four that they not only commission programmes from independent producers but also reinvest in the talent pool and business development of the independent sector.

Local authorities

Cities are centres of creativity. Creative industries will play a critical role in the revival of cities that have seen jobs in traditional industries disappear. That in turn means that one critical role for councils is to make the most of the cultural capital and capabilities of their cities. This is a difficult task for which most councils are ill-equipped. It involves both promoting a city as a centre for consumption and tourism but also helping to invest in the local production base. Politicians can provide leadership, a sense of strategy and set standards by their investment in the design of public spaces and buildings. However, they cannot impose change or direct it. It has to come from the bottom up, from an entrepreneurial spirit within a city.

Cities are developing quite different strategies to promote these new industries. However, there is still little systematic information about the scale of these cultural industries within British cities, still less the success and failure of different strategies to promote them. A useful initiative then would be to create a forum or network through which cities active in this field could share information, best practice and ideas, as well as learn from abroad.

Conclusions

The new independent cultural entrepreneurs show how a generation who were at school in the 1980s are adapting to the opportunities new technology brings but also to the reality of having to make their way in the uncertain market of the 1990s and beyond. This is just part of a much larger story of how society adapts to change. In sum, two strengths of Britain's position stand out that we need to capitalise on. The first is our historic cultural assets which leave us well placed: from English as a world language to Shakespeare, the BBC and Britain's pop music business. The second is the importance of Britain's democratic tradition in fostering these industries. These creative industries thrive in an environment that promotes openness, free speech, diversity and expression. Our capacity to breed businesses based on creative independent thought is intimately linked, in the long run, to the strength of our democratic traditions of self-governance and freedom of speech. That is why these industries are vital not just for jobs and growth but to the quality of our lives as citizens as well.

Appendix: the four cities

Glasgow

'Glasgow is a can-do city. Unless we pull ourselves up by our bootstraps we have nothing'
Michael Dale, director of the West End Festival

'I work in Glasgow because this is where my home is. It's a lifestyle choice. But commercial life is getting easier. It used to be that the BBC was only place to sell an idea. Now [we are] more able to sell ideas to different places, like Channel 4, and there is a sustainable base for talent in Glasgow. But we also have to have good links into London and not be frightened of it.'
Hamish Barbour, Ideal World Productions

'Glasgow has a huge international heritage as a City of Empire. London's so large it can be self-contained, self-referential. Glasgow has to be outward looking.'
Janice Kirkpatrick, Graven Images

'I don't know whether this argument about Glasgow and culture is a way of opening up a debate about the city's future or simple a way to disguise the city's continued crisis.'
Mel Young, publisher, The Big Issue, Scotland

The challenge

Glasgow thinks of itself as a Big Place. The city centre is laid out on a grid reminiscent of New York. The scale of the principal buildings is testimony to its past as a centre for trade in commerce and ideas. The city's capacity for innovation explains why, despite its peripheral location on a silted-up river, it became the birthplace of the steam engine and shipbuilding. In the 1990s Glasgow is trying to reinvent itself largely by playing on its creative capacity in cultural industries.[8]

Glasgow still suffers from the implosion of its traditional industries. Manufacturing employment fell by 45 per cent between 1971 and 1983 and by more than half between 1981 and 1996. Average family income is 22 per cent below the UK average. Male unemployment rates are still above the Scottish average, while economic activity is significantly below it. A very high proportion of households survive on a gross annual income of £15,000 and below. The city's population continues to decline, from 1 million in 1961 to about 620,000 in the late 1990s.

The crisis of jobs and income has brought with it a crisis of social cohesion, identity and purpose. Cultural renewal has been one element of the city's response. Glasgow is a test case for the role that cultural industries can play, not just in generating jobs but in providing a city with a renewed sense of purpose.

The local authority has played a central role in the strategy to reposition Glasgow as a post-modern city of the future. The council's attempts to rebrand the city began in the 1980s with the 'Glasgow Miles Better' campaign, which set out dispel the city's reputation as a centre for violence and drugs. That strategy moved into higher gear in 1990 when Glasgow became European City of Culture, which the city used as an opportunity to set out its stall as a centre for creativity.

Learning to be creative

There are three accounts of the impact that initiative had on Glasgow. The first is that the City of Culture year had little lasting impact. At most the event created 5,700 jobs in the arts, most of which had disappeared two years later. Although more tourists came to the city that year, the benefit was short-lived and audiences for cultural productions soon tailed off as the recession of the early 1990s took hold. For the pessimists, the attempt to reposition Glasgow as a creative city is mostly hype that disguises the high levels of poverty, unemployment and ill health that still beset the place.

A quite different account – favoured by those whose job is to promote Glasgow – is that the City of Culture sparked a renaissance in the city's economy. Almost 80 per cent of Glasgow's jobs are in financial services, telephone call centres, design, media, software and music and other services. According to the Glasgow Development Agency (GDA) and Scottish Enterprise, Glasgow is brimming with talented and ambitious entrepreneurs who are creating new companies. As Stuart Gulliver, chief executive of the GDA puts it:

'Glasgow's rich pool of creative talent is playing an increasingly crucial part in the city's successful transition from an economy largely industry based until the 1970s, to one underpinned by a vibrant mix of commerce and culture today.'

Elements of both these stories are true. The third account is that while the repositioning of Glasgow as a city of culture has not solved the city's economic and social ills, it amounts to more than hype. The 1990 initiative helped to propel a process of adaptation and learning in which public and private organisations, large and small, have developed the city's distinctive cultural assets. That process has not been straightforward or painless but it has been cumulative and reinforcing. At the end of the decade the players involved – the council, economic development agencies, the universities, broadcasters, arts institutions and entrepreneurs – have a better understanding of their task and how best to work together.

Ingredients in Glasgow's approach

One of the most important aspects of Glasgow's push into the cultural industries has been its ability to engage a diversity of players. When one source of energy has ebbed, others have flowed. Glasgow is not dependent upon one sector. The city has a base in film, television, multimedia, design and music. Different sectors have taken the lead at different times. A creative city needs strength in depth but also in diversity.

The city council is a leading investor in the cultural economy. About £70 million a year of public money goes into cultural activity in

Glasgow, about £30 million from the council. The council's leaders, in particular former leader Pat Lally, stressed that Glasgow had to 'keep on reinventing itself.' However, the push to make culture central to Glasgow's future exposed shortcomings in the council's capacity which are being addressed only now.

The council's initial approach was opportunistic and pragmatic, organised around sometimes disconnected bids to host major cultural events. The council has learned that it needs to think more strategically to generate lasting benefits from these events. The 1999 Year of Architecture and Design, for example, was organised around events but also around initiatives designed to leave a legacy: the Lighthouse Museum for architecture and design, a series of architecture projects around the city and initiatives involving schools.

The council's departments were often at odds with one another. Economic development initiatives rarely included cultural and leisure services. Even within culture and the arts there were more than ten departments, each guarding its turf. In the past two years some of these departments have been brought together in a more integrated, corporate and strategic approach.

Council executives lack knowledge of important areas of commercial cultural activity, such as music. The council realises it will have to work through partnerships and intermediaries to help develop this promising sector, which probably accounts for 3,500 jobs and an annual turnover of £100 million in the city. The Glasgow music sector combines the Scottish Opera, the Royal Scottish National Orchestra, the BBC Scottish Symphony Orchestra and Scottish Ballet as well as a host of commercial music companies: record labels such as Chemikal Underground and Limbo Record, recording studies such as CaVa and Waterfront and management companies such as Backlash Music Management. A council dominated strategy to develop this sector would almost certainly fail. Instead the council is seeking partnerships to develop the Candelriggs area of the city into a music quarter. Its aim is to help create the infrastructure for such a quarter while most of the activity within it is independent of the council.

As Bridget McConnell, Director of Culture and Leisure Services, put it in relation to libraries:

'The council's strategy has to be to act as a catalyst to mobilise all the library assets of the city, public and private and in the universities as well. That means setting strategic goals for the city as a whole, a new process of decision-making to draw together the public and private and a new organisational approach within the council.'

The council's initiative is more likely to be successful because Glasgow has a clutch of strong cultural institutions that can contribute to the process. The BBC employs 700 people in Glasgow and invests more in culture in the region than the Arts Council of Scotland. Last year almost half the 150 hours of programming it exported to the BBC network were made by independent companies. The BBC and Channel Four, through its recently established office for the regions, will play a critical role in managing the development of independent film and television production companies in Glasgow, many of which are still quite fragile. The presence of the BBC has allowed the Glasgow Development Agency to consider a plan that would turn its Pacific Quay site near the city centre into a media centre, with studios and workspace for Independents linked by a broad band communications network.

Glasgow's educational institutions, the Glasgow School of Art and the Royal College of Art, Music and Drama, help sustain the city's reputation for artistic excellence. Arts and culture courses at colleges of further education have expanded rapidly in the past few years. Most important, the city's universities – Strathclyde and Glasgow – help to attract a student population of 95,000. These institutions of higher education provide an 'intellectual highway' running through the city, in much the way that the Clyde connected the shipbuilding industry, according to Dugald Cameron, outgoing director of the Glasgow School of Art.

The economic development agencies, Scottish Enterprise and its arm in the city, the Glasgow Development Agency, although criticised by some, have a track record for developing clusters of new businesses. They have helped to create intermediaries and brokers – such as the Scottish Computer Games Alliance, Services to Software and the Glasgow Design Initiative – whose job is to help fledgling high-tech companies develop their strategy, prepare business plans and find partners. The Glasgow Design Initiative, for example, is becoming a voice for the local industry and a clearing house for ideas and contacts. Its directory lists 800 design companies in the city, with 523 consultancies, employing about 5,000 people and earning more than £225 million a year.

Glasgow's informal and amateur sector is also thriving and is a source of talent for the professional sector. There are more than 170 amateur performing societies in Glasgow, with 11,000 members and the performances they stage are equivalent to 40 per cent of the professional market.

This mix of official, institutional and informal activity has created an environment in which more cultural entrepreneurs are emerging. About 61 new design businesses have been created in Glasgow since 1996, including 26 in multimedia, for example. Employment in the music business has risen by 36 per cent in the past two years.

Impact

The cultural industries account for between 8,000 and 10,000 jobs within Glasgow, between 4 per cent and 6 per cent of the workforce. If publishing is excluded, jobs in the cultural industries increased by about 12 per cent between 1986 and 1997. Glasgow has the makings of a commercial–cultural complex, fed by relatively strong institutions of learning and economic development, political leadership that has at times set ambitious goals for the city, and a growing band of independent cultural entrepreneurs and intermediaries. The city's centre displays a dynamism and verve which is helping to breed confidence in the city's future.

However, the capacity of these industries to generate long-term benefits for all the population, non-graduates and the unskilled as well as graduates, will depend on how they help promote Glasgow as a base for other service industries – particularly financial services, call centres, retailing and leisure. The city's cultural initiatives helped to attract 1.2 million British tourists in 1997 and 540,000 overseas visitors, with a combined spend of almost £300m, accounting for more than 8 million bed nights in city hotels.

Despite recent growth, Glasgow's creative industries are fragile. The average company employs 6.5 people. Turnover of companies is high. There were sixteen new entrants into film and video between 1996 and 1998, for example, but they simply replaced the fifteen companies who exited that year. Nineteen record labels have been set up in Glasgow since 1994, but twelve others ceased trading.

The city faces immense challenges. Glasgow's population is in decline and unemployment is stubbornly above average. The local market and tax base is contracting. Only 30 per cent of Glasgow's 21 year olds have level three qualifications, against a Scottish average of 42 per cent. By European standards the city lags well behind the first division in terms of health, housing, transport and telecommunications. According to Mel Young, publisher of the Big Issue in Scotland, the magazine recruits thirteen new vendors a week in Glasgow, while in Edinburgh its vendor workforce is declining.

Prospects
Glasgow's emphasis on culture has allowed the city to punch above its weight. The players in the city's cultural sector are more aware of what they need to do, often in collaboration, to sustain Glasgow's creative reputation. The 'buzz' in the city's centre is more than superficial. However given the depths of the city's economic and social ills, especially on peripheral housing estates, it would be ridiculous to claim the cultural industries could transform the city's prospects on their own. The critical issue is how the dynamism of this sector is used to promote growth in higher quality jobs in other service sectors such as financial services, business services and software. That link has yet to be established.

Cardiff

The challenge

Cardiff faces a challenge as tough as Glasgow's. Cardiff has a population of only 290,000, the size of a British provincial city like Nottingham or Leicester. It thus has a far smaller local market for cultural producers, restaurants, clubs and galleries than Glasgow. Although Cardiff is Wales's capital city, it was awarded that status only in 1955. Cardiff is far less established than other European regional capitals – Barcelona, Marseilles, Edinburgh – to which it aspires to be compared.[9] Thus one lesson from Cardiff is that scale matters. Larger cities are likely to have more resources – both financial and cultural – than smaller cities such as Cardiff.

Cardiff is central to a much larger metropolitan area, with a combined population of almost 1.4 million, known as the Valleys, which was dominated until the 1980s by steel and coal mining. The Valleys have overshadowed Cardiff. They are the root of the area's working class politics and culture. Cardiff does not have Glasgow's sense – symbolised by Charles Rennie Mackintosh and Alexander 'Greek' Thompson – that it has a distinctive cultural heritage to live up to. Although Cardiff is a port city and in areas such as Tiger Bay has a highly cosmopolitan culture, it is less open and more parochial than either Glasgow or Liverpool.

Economic development policies have not been focused on cultural or new media industries. Instead they have been aimed at attracting inward investment from large companies to offset the decline of the traditional industries. Entrepreneurship is less prominent in Cardiff than in Manchester or Birmingham. In 1991, for example, Cardiff had only 0.72 new businesses per 1,000 people, compared to 3.9 in Manchester and 3.4 in Birmingham. 'The structure of heavy industry, often part of larger conglomerates, meant that often the brightest young people left the region rather than try to go it alone. That may be starting to change.' commented John Osmond, Director of the think tank, the Institute of Welsh Affairs.

Cardiff has the same suite of institutions as Glasgow: universities, publicly funded arts organisations, economic development agencies. Yet in Cardiff these institutions are neither as strong as in Glasgow nor as concerted, committed and knowledgeable about emerging sectors such as design and multimedia. Arts funding in Wales lags behind that in

England and the business support network is far less developed. As a consequence, the city's engagement with its cultural entrepreneurs is less effective than it could be. Thus although South Wales has a dynamic pop music scene that has spawned several well-known bands – the Manic Street Preachers, Stereophonics and Catatonia among them – it has a far less developed music industry of record labels, promoters and managers than Glasgow.

Yet Cardiff also provides at least one lesson of success. The city's strength in media highlights the critical role that broadcasters such as the BBC will play in the emerging cultural economy. Cardiff's strength in film, television and animation stems from the way that public funding for the BBC and S4C, the Welsh language channel, has helped to develop a network of independent producers. Some of these independent producers are branching out from television into multimedia.

The setting

Arts and cultural industries employ about 28,600 people in Wales, 2.6 per cent of the workforce. Many of these jobs are part-time and casual, often within micro-businesses. The sector has a turnover of about £836 million and spends an additional £300 million on other services, thus generating a further 2,000 jobs. With a growth rate of 5 per cent a year, one in twenty of the Welsh workforce would be employed in these industries by the year 2020. The sector's job-generating capacity stems from the high levels of trade within the sector. Between 20 and 40 per cent of sales are made to other cultural organisations. The Welsh Development Agency estimates that an extra £1 million of turnover in the cultural industries generates 100 jobs in those industries and a further 74 jobs in related industries.

A majority of these cultural sector jobs are in south east Wales. According to Phil Cooke, director of the Centre for Advanced Studies at Cardiff University, the city has an employed workforce of about 170,000, with about 10,000 in cultural, creative and media jobs, about 7 per cent. Cardiff is home to at least 326 recognised cultural business, which together employ about 2,929 people, with about 1,865 self-employed producers. A further 2,000 jobs probably depend upon this employment within the cultural industries. The cultural industries thus make up a small but increasingly significant sector within the Cardiff economy.

The institutions
Cardiff has many of the institutions a city requires to develop a dynamic cultural economy. However, the city also shows that what really matters is how these institutions interact with one another and the local economy.

The number of university students in Cardiff has expanded from 14,700, in the mid-1980s, to more than 17,000 in the late 1990s. However by contrast Rennes, a French city of about 200,000 people, has 37,500 students. Barcelona has 134,000 students, almost a tenth of its population. In Cardiff students make up one in twenty of the population. Cardiff is less of a student city than either Manchester or Glasgow. It has a smaller market for cheap, experimental culture and probably attracts and retains a lower share of young people than other cities.

Cardiff has some strong specialist institutions of arts education, notably the Welsh College of Music and Drama and the University of Cardiff Institute, which together produce several hundred trained performers and creators each year. However, a recent review of the role of these institutions notes:

'These institutions are only now beginning to pay attention to the link between their provision and the economy of the sector in the city. There remains little direct contact between the industry and education, no strategy for the retention of the best talent in the city after graduation and little enterprise training to equip graduates for entry into the economy.'[10]

The city council has an important role to play, mainly by running the St David's Concert Hall in the city centre and by disbursing grants worth about £500,000 a year to community arts organisations. Although the city has an arts strategy it is far less ambitious than Glasgow's and less integrated with plans for economic development. The Arts Council of Wales has started to show greater interest in the economic potential of the arts, but its traditional role has been to fund large, stable organisations and institutions. There is little funding for individuals and entrepreneurs.

As a capital city, Cardiff is home to many of Wales' national cultural institutions, including the National Orchestra of Wales, the Welsh National Opera and a clutch of national museums. These institutions are vital for a small, relatively young nation, as a focal point for a distinctive national culture. However they are also expensive. The four national museums in Cardiff receive between £7 million and £10 million of state support and the Welsh National Opera receives between £5 million and £7.5 million. The National Orchestra of Wales would not exist without the BBC's backing. The main role of these national institutions is to deliver publicly sponsored culture to the region. They are not well integrated into a local production base.

Indeed during our interviews in Cardiff, people both young and old were far more likely to mention the success of Manic Street Preachers and Stereophonics as a symbol of a vibrant national culture of which they could be proud. The South Wales pop music scene has a strong but informal organisation, around a few key venues, some influential managers and Internet sites such as Virtual Cardiff, which takes more than 45,000 hits a week. The very success of these local bands, however, only underlines the lack of an indigenous music industry capable of making the most of this local talent. South Wales, in contrast to Glasgow and Manchester, is strong on talent but weak on the business infrastructure to make the most of it. Most of the earnings generated by these bands go to record labels and managers based in London.

Wales, like Scotland, has long had a distinctive approach to economic development focused around the Welsh Development Agency (WDA). The presence of an economic development agency with resources to match its local knowledge should give Cardiff an advantage in developing its cultural economy. The WDA is developing its role in this area. For example, in conjunction with the Cardiff Bay Development Corporation and Screen Wales it has set up a Multimedia Development Group to address the development of new media industries in Wales. However, the WDA is largely known for attracting large inward investment projects designed to revive manufacturing employment in the region. The agency is less used to dealing with service and software-based sectors populated by a large number of smaller, indigenous companies.

One indication of how much further Cardiff has to go to promote itself as a creative, cultural city is its relatively poor performance in tourism. The city's hotel bed-space occupancy rate is low at 34 per cent. Cardiff has 10 per cent of Wales's population but attracts only 1.2 per cent of Wales's 46.4 million tourist bed-nights a year. Cardiff's ratio of tourists per head of population is 2.3, compared with 9 in Edinburgh, 5.7 in Amsterdam and 7.9 in Manchester.

Media

Although Cardiff lacks the cultural dynamism of Glasgow and Manchester it has one area of outstanding strength: the media. This is a prime example of how a combination of public funding, deregulation, robust institutions and entrepreneurship have combined to create a relatively healthy production base within the city.

The public policy commitment that Wales should be served by its own broadcasters – BBC Wales and S4C – has paid dividends in the past decade and a half by helping to create a body of independent producers around the city. Most of these businesses serve the broadcasters. Yet in the past few years the Cardiff media cluster has started to develop specialities, such as animation, and it has begun to spread into new areas of computer games and multimedia.

In the 1980s there were perhaps no more than 40 media companies – independent producers and post-production houses – clustered around the Cardiff broadcasters. But since then there has been dramatic growth in the number of independents, fuelled by the broadcasters deciding to commission more programmes from independents as well as by new entrants moving into the expanding multimedia sector of video, film, computer graphics, CD-roms and Internet software.

According to a report by Philip Cooke and Gwawr Hughes at the University of Wales, in the late 1990s more than 300 companies in the Cardiff area were involved in media, animation, graphics and support services and employed at least 2,000 workers with a combined turnover of about £90 million. About 57 per cent of these businesses employed between one and five people and 63 per cent had a turnover of less than £500,000. The growth of employment among the small Independents has more than offset the decline in employment among the larger broadcasters. The future prospects of the sector no long rely on the broadcasters alone, although they are critical players. The media sector in Cardiff depends on the strengths and weaknesses of a mini-agglomeration of small companies that need to diversify into new markets and technologies where they are less reliant upon the broadcasters.

The report concludes:

'While the industry remains relatively small by the global standards of the industry centred in California and London, it is, nevertheless, relatively robust, creative and dynamic yet largely cooperatively-minded and flexible enough to remain competitive.'[11]

BBC Wales is one lynchpin of this agglomeration. The BBC spends £66 million a year on productions based in Wales and plays a critical role in providing stability to this relatively fragile sector. BBC Wales has an annual turnover of £80 million and employs 1,000 staff. It largely sustains Wales's only professional orchestra and invests more in Welsh cultural production than the Arts Council of Wales. BBC Cardiff was recently designated a centre of excellence for music production and has embarked on a five year strategy to develop the local production base, including festivals such as Cardiff Singer of the World and a proposed world festival of theatre music. Although the BBC is sometimes criticised by Independents for being too slow moving, it will be vital to the development of the independent sector, particularly as its own strategy takes it into digital television and on-line services.

The BBC is also the largest single programme provider to S4C, which was launched in 1982. The BBC provides a third of S4C's Welsh language output, eight of its ten most watched programmes and all of its schools output. S4C, which is funded through the Department of Culture, Media and Sport in London, is also a critical investor in the local cultural economy. S4C's critics argue it spends quite large sums – an annual income of £70 million largely from the government – on fairly small audiences: only 19 per cent of people in Wales are Welsh speakers. The channel's advocates argue that its significance extends beyond its viewing figures to the sustenance of Welsh language and culture. Welsh language pop bands such as Catatonia kept going before becoming famous in part thanks to S4C's patronage. Cardiff's cluster of animators – the likes of Joanna Quinn and Deiniol Morris – have developed in part thanks to Chris Grace, head of animation at S4C, who is an exemplary cultural entrepreneur. Grace has used the public fund available to S4C to invest in local producers, attract foreign finance for projects and broker deals for the production and distribution of large-scale international projects, such as the award winning animated Canterbury Tales. The BBC invested nearly £2.5 million in these animation projects.

The connections between the BBC and S4C to an indigenous production base, combined with the recently created Screen Wales to finance film production, are strong enough to allow Cardiff's media cluster to grow and develop as technologies and markets change. Indeed, Cardiff's relative strength in new and old media only serves to highlight its weakness in other fields of cultural entrepreneurship.

John Osmond, of the Institute for Welsh Affairs, sums up the situation thus:

'Culture and particularly the media – BBC Wales and S4C – have helped to define Welshness in a civic sense because Wales lacks many of the distinctive traditions of law and education that Scotland has. But we are only just moving out of a situation in which Wales was too heavily dependent on English and in particular, London, patronage. The big industries of South Wales – steel and coal – were British Steel and British Coal. Through the trade unions and the Labour party the region was wrapped into a dependent relationship with London. With the combination of industrial change and political devolution we are entering a new era but we are just at the outset.'

Michelle Ryan, one of the co-founders of Telessyn, the film and television production cooperative, makes the same point but in a different way:

'For too long we have had an apologetic culture because we are too close to London. It is very difficult to represent Wales in a more modern, dynamic way. Most of the country is rural: Cardiff does not represent it. We do not have the urban culture of Manchester or Glasgow. The Welsh language gives some people a cultural anchor, but it can be very closed and inward looking, people just talking to one another and not to the outside world. Creating an English language Welsh identity is far more problematic, given how much our culture and politics is wrapped into London. That is why cultural renewal and dynamism will only really take off with some visionary political leadership, not a cautious, municipal, managerialism of the kind we are all too used to.'

Brighton

'We do what we do because we enjoy it, it's not just a job, it's a lifestyle and that is probably true of most people who work with us or for us. Brighton is like St Ives, it's an artists retreat. Clients from large companies love coming here. They love the sea, the restaurants. It's lively.'
Peter Barker, Desktop Displays

The lifestyle economy
Brighton has always had a close but ambivalent relationship with London. The seaside town and its environs have long been a popular destination for London day-trippers and summer tourists, from the Prince Regent onwards, and a small colony of artists and writers who mainly worked in London. The nickname – 'London by the Sea' – suggested Brighton was little more than a distant suburb of the capital. Although Brighton is home to the largest mixed-arts festival in England (the Brighton Festival), it has no repertory theatre, only one small arts cinema and a dearth of venues for everything from small bands to arts galleries.

In the past few years, however, the 'London by the Sea' tag has been embraced. It suggests that Brighton is a cosmopolitan, diverse, even metropolitan place, which offers a higher quality of life than London. Design consultant Johnny Shipp, who lives in Brighton and works there as well as in London, says Brighton shares much with London but has little in common with the South East. He argues the town should celebrate its proximity to the city: 'It should be on the tube map.'

Lifestyle is the main reason businesses locate in Brighton, especially new media and cultural business. A survey by the consultancy Human Capital found that more than 70 per cent of media companies in the South East were there because that was where the owner chose to live.

Writer and broadcaster Simon Fanshawe argues that this is particularly true of Brighton which is a good host to eccentricity – it has a large gay and lesbian population – and birthplace for 'lifestyle' businesses such as the shoe shop Pied á Terre, Infinity Foods health foods and the Body Shop. Fanshawe is sanguine that many of Brighton's artistic community work elsewhere most of the time.

'There is a large artistic community in Brighton which can support local ventures and bring in skills from wider worlds. You couldn't draw on that range of skills in every town and its proximity to London helps. But it's not London and that is what gives it its special feel, because people *choose* to live here.'

In respects it is unfair and unhelpful to compare Brighton with a much larger city, like Glasgow, with a quite different history. Indeed one of the main findings of our research, borne out by Brighton, is that cities have to find their own niche, based on their distinctive strengths. There is no easy model to follow. Brighton, for a town its size, has a large, lively cultural community. It may seem fragile compared with that of Glasgow or London, but it is thriving compared with other seaside towns with relatively old populations such as Eastbourne or Bournemouth. This cultural community is dominated by self-employed freelancers and small businesses, many of which are fragile. However, it could yet promote a large Internet company or a computer games maker. So although it would be over-egging Brighton's pudding to describe it as the San Francisco of the south coast, it is better placed than many towns of its size to engage in the new economy.

New media and visual arts

'The universities matter. There are more smaller new media companies. Some people who used to work here have just set up a business to do computer modelling. In virtually every area we have a local option when we need to call on a supplier or pull in a freelancer. Every marginal step forward strengthens the local base and increases the likelihood that eventually something will happen.'
Alex Morrison, managing director, Cognitive Applications

There is very little data on the extent of the cultural industries in Brighton but in two areas – fine arts and new media – Brighton is home to a cluster of Independents. Wired Sussex, a trade body, estimates there are about 350 new media companies in Sussex, about half of them in Brighton and Hove. The majority of these companies employ less than ten people, though a few are larger: Maxim Training and Epic both employ about 100 people.

The consultancy Human Capital argues that new media is significant in the Brighton area in part because traditional media, film and television are relatively small. Brighton does not have a television broadcaster and there are only a handful of independent production companies. Human Capital argues that new media companies providing corporate website design and production are as significant as television production companies, while leisure software, such as computer games, is more significant than either film or television in the local economy.

Brighton has a high concentration of visual artists working in fine art, applied art and design. Many in Brighton claim the town has the largest cluster of visual artists outside Hoxton and Hackney in East London. The only hard evidence to back up this claim is that the town's twenty studios, which offer about 300 spaces, are full. Many artists work from home: more than 350 of them exhibit work from home in the 'Open House' events which are part of the Brighton Festival.

However, as with other cities, Brighton has found it difficult to turn a thriving cultural scene into a thriving local industry.

Lifestyle entrepreneurs
Many of Brighton's cultural entrepreneurs have a carefully cultivated, 'non-commercial' outlook. Despite the presence of a few larger companies, such as Epic Multimedia or Maxim Training, many new media companies intend to remain relatively small. As Alex Morrison of Cognitive Applications explained, quality of work is what interests him, not size of company. Peter Barker of Desktop Displays questioned whether there was any advantage to organisational size in an industry which he felt had no economies of scale.

Brighton's new media industry is a micro-economy of service companies. Alan Cawson, Professor of Multimedia at Sussex University and an investor in new media companies, argues it will be hard for Brighton-based companies to grow because few have products that can provide a decent revenue stream. Others are looking for grants and public funds, which militates against 'entrepreneurial solutions' he says.

Many companies claim they do not want to invest in growth because they will have to 'give too much away' if they accept venture capital or other outside investment. But Cawson argues that many small companies do not look for outside investment because they are happy to grow organically and keen to retain control.

While there is some joint project working among Brighton companies there is less trade between the companies than in London's Soho for example or even within Cardiff's media cluster. Indeed most Brighton producers have to leave town to find clients. Nor has Brighton attracted significant inward investment from large companies.

The strength, but also the weakness, of the local economy is its reliance upon freelancers and independents. The local economy is adaptive but fragile. Fred Hasson, of interactive TV company Victoria Real, is developing a network for new media companies with growth potential in the South East, a post funded by the Government Office for the South East. Hasson says the general skill level in Brighton is good:

'There are lots of people with programming and web design skills, but they don't realise that these skills are not enough, soon everyone will be able to do these things. They just want to get on with designing their websites and content while the business is moving on around them.'

Educational institutions

Both the University of Sussex and Brighton University play an important role in the town's cultural industries. The universities, together with the town's language schools, make education the largest sector in the Brighton economy. There are between 17,000 and 20,000 students in Brighton.

The University of Sussex's Cognitive Studies Department is responsible for many of the skilled graduates who populate the local multimedia economy. Its role in the new media industry can't be overstated. As well as cognitive studies, which combines linguistics, psychology, artificial intelligence and computer sciences, Sussex also runs a well-respected media studies degree. Brighton University offers degrees in design, fashion and fine arts, and many of the towns visual artists are its graduates. The Innovation Centre, a business incubator for high technology companies, funded by the universities, has a waiting list of applicants.

Public policy
Public policy led by the local authority has played a far less significant role in Brighton than in other cities such as Glasgow and Sheffield. Dave Reeves of Zap Productions argued that Brighton council had only recently woken up to the cultural activity on its doorstep.

The council's budget is limited. Paula Murray, project manager for arts and leisure in Brighton and Hove Council, has a direct budget of only £300,000 and her main role is as a broker identifying opportunities, filling in lottery applications, encouraging networking and so on. As part of the relatively prosperous South East, Brighton is not in a position to claim the European Union structural fund grants available to cities in less prosperous areas such as Cardiff and Glasgow.

Institutions that receive support from the council – the Brighton Media Centre for example – often find the support is in kind rather than in cash. Ian Elwick of the Brighton Media Centre, a managed workspace for media companies, said the centre had to rely on self-help, whereas in other towns such as Huddersfield the local authority has played a more central role.

Some feel this is a strength: many developments in Brighton are grassroots initiatives rather than being directed from above. One such initiative is Fabrica, an artist-led gallery in an old church in the centre of Brighton. This brainchild of artists from Red Herring studios was established in 1995 with a three year grant from the Single Regeneration Budget. Although the economic development department of the council helped in securing the money, Debbie Barker, the gallery's administrator, feels Brighton has been less active than other towns in developing and projecting its cultural industries.

Workspace and venues continue to be a problem in Brighton. Lottery funding will allow the town to redevelop the Dome Theatre as a touring venue but it lacks the range of other venues to exhibit art or host performances that a city such as Glasgow has. Although the Brighton's nightclub economy is thriving, this dominates the largest venues in the city. Brighton's development is constrained by the sea on one side and the Sussex Downs on the other. As Tim Cornish of South East Arts points out, unlike former industrial cities Brighton does not have many decaying factories and warehouses in which to cluster small businesses.

Although the private rented sector is large and there is spare office space, cheap workspace is increasingly hard to find.

Conclusion

Brighton is making a virtue of necessity. It is not so much a cultural industrial economy but a cultural lifestyle economy. While there are institutional weaknesses, grassroots initiatives have sprung up. Where there is little public funding, small-scale initiatives and self-help develop. The question mark that hangs over these admirably adaptive strategies is their lack of ambition. Many people working in Brighton are happy to be dependent upon London for work and income, as long as they can retain the distinctive feel of life in Brighton. They can tick over, hoping to ride each wave of new technology but most are not aiming to do much more than that.

Nevertheless, as a seaside town Brighton would be even more heavily dependent upon tourism and conferences if it did not have a lively cultural economy. It is better placed than many towns of similar size to stand a chance of participating in the new economy.

Sheffield

The challenge

Sheffield is seen by many as a pioneer in the development of cultural industries' policies. The council was one of the first to identify the potential of the cultural industries when it targeted their development in the early 1980s in the teeth of a fierce recession in the city's main steel, mining and engineering industries. The city is one test case of how public policy led investment in cultural production can help to alleviate the decline in a city's traditional industries.

The Greater London Council had embarked on similar work, but it started from a stronger, richer base. Sheffield was a provincial, industrial city, without a regional broadcasting base. Sheffield does not have Glasgow's inspiring built environment, nor its history as a centre of global trade and ideas. Sheffield had always been good at producing pop groups and singers, from Joe Cocker in the 1960s to his name sake Jarvis in the 1990s, by way of Human League. Yet too much local talent migrated swiftly to London.

To stop the rot, the council took a bold strategic move to develop its cultural industries to help to diversify the city's economy. Sheffield's strategy is production led, an echo of its strong manufacturing culture. Sheffield put its emphasis on building up a production base in the rather than attempting to attract tourism and leisure industries around clubs, bars, cafes and restaurants. To achieve this goal the city council's Department of Employment and Economic Development, (DEED) took a leading role that focused on the development of the cultural industries quarter as a production centre.

The cultural industries quarter

The opening of the Leadmill Arts Centre and the Yorkshire Artspace Society in 1980, followed in 1986 by Red Tape studios, marked the beginning of a process of developing cultural production which today is known as the Cultural Industries Quarter (CIQ), a former industrial area on the edge of the city centre.

A 1997 report on the CIQ, commissioned by the council and its partners in the venture, found that the quarter had received a cumulative investment of £35 million over more than ten years resulting in:

- over 150 cultural businesses in music, film, video, broadcasting, design and photography
- turnover in excess of £20 million per year and between 1,300 and 1,400 jobs
- 1,500 media training places a year
- an associated infrastructure and business support services that should be of lasting value to the city.

Film, video and music businesses account for about 30 per cent of cultural businesses in the quarter. About 75 per cent of companies employ ten people or less and only 5 per cent employ more than 25. Gremlin, the computer games maker and the largest cultural employer in the city, is outside the formal Quarter.

Critics argue the CIQ is small and in respects marginal to the rest of the Sheffield economy. Its supporters argue that Sheffield was starting from a very low level and only now does it have a base from which it can grow. Although Sheffield has two large universities and a large student population, it has lacked other cultural institutions – such as a local broadcaster – that have fed the cultural industries in other cities. Sheffield's public investment in cultural industries highlights why cultural production and consumption are best developed in tandem and why public policy alone cannot create a thriving cultural industries sector within a city: private entrepreneurship is also required.

Debate about the role of the CIQ centres on the degree to which it is integrated into Sheffield life. Even advocates of the quarter admit that the focus on building up production industries meant that the public had to wait a long time before there was much visible benefit for them in terms of cultural consumption. The opening of the Showroom Cinema at the end of the Workstation building, a former car showroom and, more recently, the National Centre for Popular Music (NCPM) has given the area a couple of a large attractions. Yet it remains cut off from the rest of the city centre, not least by Sheffield's notoriously tricky road system. A café–bar and a couple of small restaurants have sprung up, but the area is mainly quiet at night.

Ian Wild, manager of the Showroom Cinema and a graduate of DEED, says the council did not 'market' the CIQ for fear of over-hyping the development. The Showroom is one of the largest arts cinemas outside

London, a more glamorous successor to the small municipal arts cinema, The Anvil, which closed in 1991. The Showroom only opened in 1995 after protracted debate and acquired its third and fourth screens only with the help of lottery funding. Wild says the Showroom provides a showcase for foreign language and special interest films and documentaries. Critics argue the Showroom caters only for a minority.

The DEED's role in promoting the quarter – and in particular a small group within the department – has provoked criticism that a clique dominates the quarter. Moira Sutton, former manager of the Red Tape record label called it a 'boys club': 'All the same people are involved in everything. Although this is not as much the case as it used to be – it has left a bad taste.' Anthony Waller, now Director of Dance Agency Cornwall, but formerly in Sheffield, acknowledged that apart from a few key people in and around the department most politicians and council officials were disparaging about the CIQ until the National Centre for Popular Music got its Lottery funding. Many hope the creation of a Cultural Industries Development Agency in the city will be a chance to bring in fresh blood.

Many people seem to believe the quarter has not fully exploited its potential for networking. Moira Sutton, now a consultant to media companies, acknowledges there is some inter-company working within the quarter but 'it is not in any constructive sense, a network.' On the contrary, she says, the CIQ 'is phenomenally factionalised with low levels of trust and a culture of subsidy dependency. Networking even between natural allies does not happen, people get together in the pub, but it doesn't lead to very much.'

Although many, including Moira Sutton, worry that the businesses within the CIQ are fragile and many could not survive without public support, most people involved with cultural industries in the region believe the CIQ has helped strengthen the local skills base. 'The technical skills base, especially in music technology and film, is very much better than it was ten years ago,' she says. 'The thing that is horribly missing is business acumen and basic people management skills. Some companies were supported well beyond their sell-by date.'

Conclusion

Sheffield's story shows how far public policy can go in promoting local cultural industries but also its limits. In the midst of the sharp decline in Sheffield's traditional industries, the council was virtually the only actor that could address local economic development in a concerted fashion. Sheffield does not have a broadcaster and lacks some of the cultural institutions that other cities could draw on. It has to compete with Leeds, 40 miles to the north, which is rebranding itself as a 24 hour student city, and the lure of London for its talented young people. Set against this backdrop of economic dislocation, institutional weakness and lack of indigenous entrepreneurship, Sheffield's achievements are modest but impressive. The retention of a local skills base in these industries is a significant achievement and although Gremlin, the computer games company, is not part of the CIQ it reports no difficulties in recruiting local talent, in part because the CIQ has helped to develop it.

Sylvia Harvey of Sheffield Hallam University, whose original work in the 1980s led to the development of the CIQ, reflected:

'Things have improved, particularly in film and TV production. Nevertheless, Sheffield remains the biggest city in England without a TV station and without a broadcaster it is difficult to build or sustain independent production. It is immensely difficult to grow a sector, it takes a long time. It has been a long, slow process to grow something quite small, but even though it is small it is rooted here.'

However, the Sheffield strategy also highlights the limits of relying on public policy to drive development in these industries. The emphasis on production, as the expense of consumption, means the links between the two are probably under-exploited. Dynamic clusters need to be open to new entrants who drive change, yet the reliance on a small team from the DEED has exposed the initiative to accusations of élitism. The dependence on public money to support the Cultural Industries Quarter means too few of the businesses are self-sustaining or entrepreneurial in outlook.

Notes

1. *The Creative Industries Task Force Mapping Report*, Department for Culture, Media and Sport, October 1998, and mapping exercise prepared by Spectrum Strategy Consultants, February 1998.

2. *Cultural Production in Manchester: Research and Strategy*, report prepared by Justin O'Connor, Manchester Institute of Popular Culture, 1999.

3. This point is made by Angela McRobbie in her account of the lives of young fashion designers: *British Fashion Design; Rag Trade or Image Industry* Routledge, London, 1998. See also *Recommendations for growth: UK Digital Media,* Digital Media Alliance report, available from Arts Council of England, prepared by Catalyst Media.

4. The role of cities as centres of creativity and innovation is highlighted in: Hall P, 1998, *Cities and Civilization* , Weidenfeld and Nicolson, London; *The Richness of Cities* working papers, published by Comedia in association with Demos in 1998 and 1999; Landry C and Bianchini F, 1995, *The Creative City*, Demos, London; 'Cultural Industries and the City', presentation to European Union Culture Ministers, March 1998, Manchester Institute of Popular Culture.

5. Many of the figures in this section are drawn from *Cultural Production in Manchester* (see note 2) and its analysis of official statistics.

6. For example see Pratt A, *The Cultural Industries Sector: its definition and character from secondary sources on employment and trade, Britain 1984-91*, London School of Economics Research Paper No 41, LSE, London, and Pratt A, 1999, *Employment in the Creative Industries in Scotland*, report for Scottish Enterprise.

7. O'Brien J and Feist A, *Employment in the Arts and Cultural Industries: An analysis of the 1991 census*, Arts Council of England.

8. This profile of Glasgow drew on many sources, among them. *Metropolitan Glasgow: Creative city*, Glasgow Development Agency, 1999; *Glasgow Cultural Statistics Framework*, Glasgow City Council, 1998; *Music Strategy for the City of Glasgow*, report prepared for Glasgow City Council by Comedia with Roger Tym and Partners, with the Institute of Popular Culture, November 1998; *Creative Scotland: The case for a national cultural strategy*, prepared by Comedia for the National Cultural Agencies of Scotland and the Convention of Scottish Local Authorities, published by the Scottish Arts Council; *Glasgow's Renewed Prosperity, Consultation Document*, Glasgow Development Agency, January 1999.

9. This profile of Cardiff was pre-
pared with the help of among others
these sources: *Cardiff Making a
European City of the Future*, Report
Commissioned by South Glamorgan
County Council, Philip Cooke,
Professor of City and Regional
Planning, University of Wales College
of Cardiff; *Cardiff EuroCity*, A report
prepared by Coopers and Lybrand for
the Institute of Welsh Affairs; *Arts and
Cultural Industries in Regional
Development*, Arts Council of Wales,
December 1998; *State of the Arts*, David
Clarke, Institute of Welsh Affairs,
1998; *The Economic Impact of the Arts and
Cultural Industries in Wales*, Welsh
Economic Research Unit, University of
Cardiff Business School, November
1998; *Culture Innovation and Economy in
Cardiff*, Centre for Advanced Studies,
University of Wales, Cardiff, May
1996; *The Emerging Multimedia Cluster in
Cardiff Bay*, Philip Cooke and Gawr
Hughes, Centre for Advanced Studies,
University of Wales, Cardiff, January
1998.

10. *Culture Innovation and Economy in
Cardiff*, Centre for Advanced Studies,
University of Wales, Cardiff, May
1996.

11. Cook and Hughes, 1998 (see note 9).